RUSSIA
in Pictures

Herón Márquez

Lerner Publications Company

Contents

Website address: www.lernerbooks.com

Lerner Publications Company
A division of Lerner Publishing Group
241 First Avenue North
Minneapolis, MN 55401 U.S.A.

web enhanced @ www.vgsbooks.com

CULTURAL LIFE — 48

► Religion. Holidays and Festivals. Literature. Music and Dance. Visual Arts and Architecture. Sports and Recreation. Food.

THE ECONOMY — 58

► Services, Industry, and Energy. Agriculture, Forestry, and Fishing. Foreign Trade. Illegal Activities. The Future.

FOR MORE INFORMATION

Library of Congress Cataloging-in-Publication Data

Márquez, Herón.
      Russia in pictures / Herón Márquez.—Rev. and expanded.
          p.   cm. — (Visual geography series)
      Includes bibliographical references and index.
      ISBN: 0-8225-0937-7 (lib. bdg. : alk. paper)
          1. Russia—Pictorial works—Juvenile literature. 2. Soviet Union—Pictorial works—Juvenile literature.
      3. Russia (Federation)—Pictorial works—Juvenile literature. I. Title. II. Visual geography series
      (Minneapolis, Minn.)
      DK18.5.M37 2004
      947—dc21   2003003557

Manufactured in the United States of America
1 2 3 4 5 6 - JR - 09 08 07 06 05 04

INTRODUCTION

Russia has always seemed larger than life. Given the size and the history of the country, it is easy to see why. Modern Russia began in the A.D. 800s as a humble collection of villages in eastern Europe. Over the centuries, Russia became a powerful monarchy and expanded across Asia to the Pacific Ocean and beyond, establishing one of the great empires of the world. Russian emperors, called czars, held their vast empire together through wars, invasions, and internal disunity.

But that unity came at great cost to the nation's peasants. These farm laborers provided Russia with raw materials but bore the brunt of hard times. In the early part of the twentieth century, the country's political, social, and economic pressures exploded in the Russian Revolution and resulted in the end of the ancient monarchy. Led by Vladimir Ilich Lenin, revolutionaries took control of the country and founded the Union of Soviet Socialist Republics (USSR), a nation made up of Russia and surrounding states. The USSR was a Communist nation—the first in history. Under this political and economic system,

the government (in the people's name) took ownership of all property and controlled virtually every facet of life. In return, the government pledged to distribute wealth more evenly and to improve living standards for the vast majority of the nation's people. But Communist leaders abused their power. They crushed opposition to their control, killed and imprisoned their own people, and did little for the poor to whom they'd promised so much.

Lenin was followed by Joseph Stalin, who ruled ruthlessly for three decades. Stalin's desire for power transformed the country from an agricultural state into one of the mightiest industrial and military nations in the world. But Stalin's drive for power and expansion resulted in the death and imprisonment of millions.

Communist rule finally ended under Mikhail Gorbachev. Gorbachev tried to reform the Communist Party and Soviet society. But instead of saving the Soviet Union, Gorbachev's reforms led to its demise. The Soviet Union collapsed in 1991.

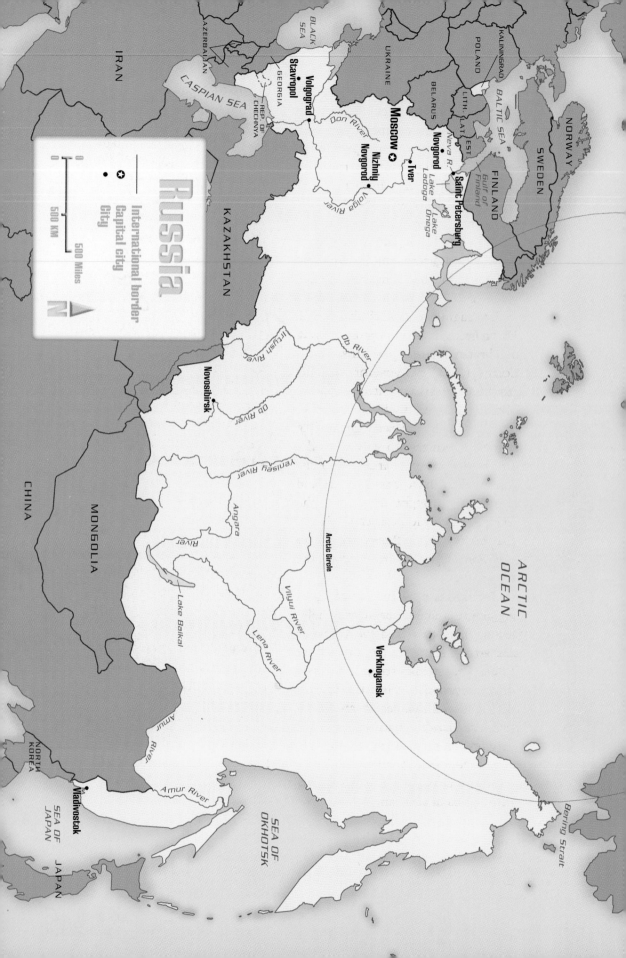

Following the USSR's fall, Russia remained the largest country in the world, but it faced incredible economic and political problems. Seeking stability and strength, it joined some of the former Soviet republics to become the Russian Federation. Along with a new name, Russia's people sought a new way of life. They began to enjoy rights and freedoms that had long been denied to them.

Although the end of the Soviet Union brought greater opportunity, it also brought greater problems. Under Communism, the government had provided everything from jobs to homes. After the breakup, Russians felt as though they were competing against one another to survive. In the late 1990s, a major financial crisis, combined with increasing crime and corruption, brought Russia to the brink of economic disaster. Civil war also broke out, as Russia sought to keep some republics from leaving the federation.

Through a combination of internal reforms and international help, Russia had stabilized its economy and government by the end of the 1990s. Despite the struggles, Russia has great promise. It is home to more than 140 million people and more than one hundred nationalities. The country possesses some of the largest deposits of oil, natural gas, and coal in the world. These resources may help restore Russia to good economic health after many years of suffering.

DIFFERING DATES

Why do Russians celebrate the October Revolution in November? Why is Christmas in January? These date discrepancies occur because Russia has used two different calendars. The Gregorian calendar was created in the 1500s to replace the older, less accurate Julian calendar. By the 1700s, most of the world was using the Gregorian calendar. Russia, however, did not switch until 1918. At that point, the Julian calendar was fourteen days behind the Gregorian calendar. So when the switch was made on January 31, 1918, the next day became February 14. The October Revolution, which took place on October 25, is celebrated on November 7. Because the Russian Orthodox Church refused to switch, Russians celebrate Christmas on January 7 instead of December 25. In this book, all dates reflect the Gregorian calendar.

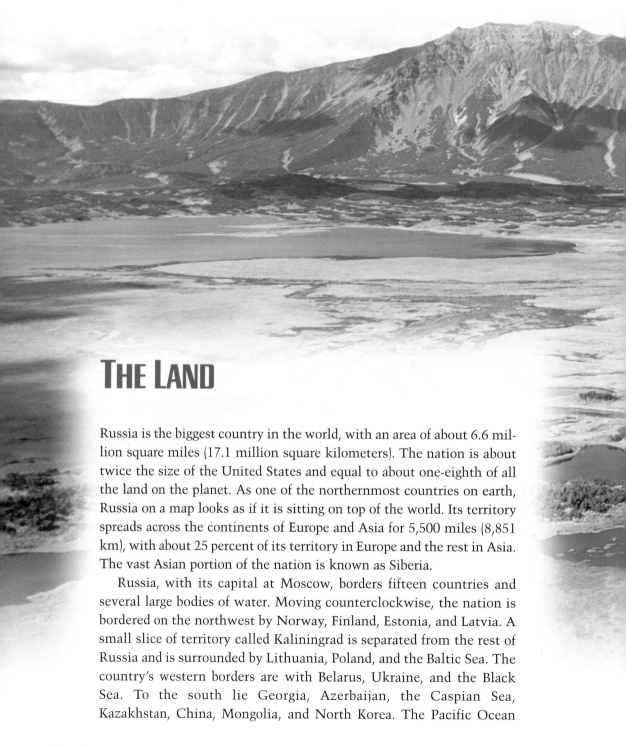

THE LAND

Russia is the biggest country in the world, with an area of about 6.6 million square miles (17.1 million square kilometers). The nation is about twice the size of the United States and equal to about one-eighth of all the land on the planet. As one of the northernmost countries on earth, Russia on a map looks as if it is sitting on top of the world. Its territory spreads across the continents of Europe and Asia for 5,500 miles (8,851 km), with about 25 percent of its territory in Europe and the rest in Asia. The vast Asian portion of the nation is known as Siberia.

Russia, with its capital at Moscow, borders fifteen countries and several large bodies of water. Moving counterclockwise, the nation is bordered on the northwest by Norway, Finland, Estonia, and Latvia. A small slice of territory called Kaliningrad is separated from the rest of Russia and is surrounded by Lithuania, Poland, and the Baltic Sea. The country's western borders are with Belarus, Ukraine, and the Black Sea. To the south lie Georgia, Azerbaijan, the Caspian Sea, Kazakhstan, China, Mongolia, and North Korea. The Pacific Ocean

and the Sea of Okhotsk wash Russia's eastern shores, and Japan lies across the Sea of Japan. Russia's chilly north is bounded by the Arctic Ocean, and the U.S. state of Alaska is only about 50 miles (80 km) away from Russia's far northeastern border across the Bering Strait.

Topography

Russia's land, varying widely in its features and conditions, can be broken down in many different ways. One way to study the land is to look at its four broad vegetation zones: the tundra, the taiga, the steppes, and the desert.

Located in Russia's far north, the tundra is a permanently frozen, treeless, usually snow-covered expanse. Located almost entirely inside the Arctic Circle (an imaginary line at a far northern latitude on the globe), the tundra stretches along the shores of the Arctic Ocean.

This windswept region gradually transforms into an enormous stretch of evergreen forest, called the taiga, that covers about half of

Russia. South of the taiga are the broad, grassy plains, or steppes, of Russia. Finally, in the far southwestern corner of the steppes, near the Caspian Sea, is a small, arid stretch of desert.

In addition to these vegetation zones, topographical features also break up Russia's landscape. The country's most important topographical regions are its steppes, plateaus, and mountains.

STEPPES As both a vegetation zone and a topographical feature, the Russian steppes are the nation's most important land feature. These plains form the heart of Russia and provide the nation's best agricultural land, much of it covered by a rich, dark soil called chernozem (black earth). The fertile chernozem is formed by the growth and decay of grasses covering the steppes.

The steppes stretch from the Polish border in the west to the Yenisey River—a waterway flowing northward through Siberia to the Arctic Ocean—in the east. The grasslands located west of the Ural Mountains are on the Russian Plain, part of the larger European Plain that begins at the Baltic Sea and extends eastward. The Russian Plain does not rise much more than 600 feet (183 meters) above sea level. It is the historic core of Russia and home to about 75 percent of the country's population of 143.5 million. The steppes east of the Urals are part of the West Siberian Plain. This plain covers an area of more than 1 million square miles (2.6 million sq. km), rising no higher than 500 feet (152 m) above sea level. Because of harsh weather, this plain is either marshy or frozen most of the year.

A rancher rounds up a herd of cattle near his farm in Stavropol on the **Russian steppes.** This fertile area is home to many of Russia's farms.

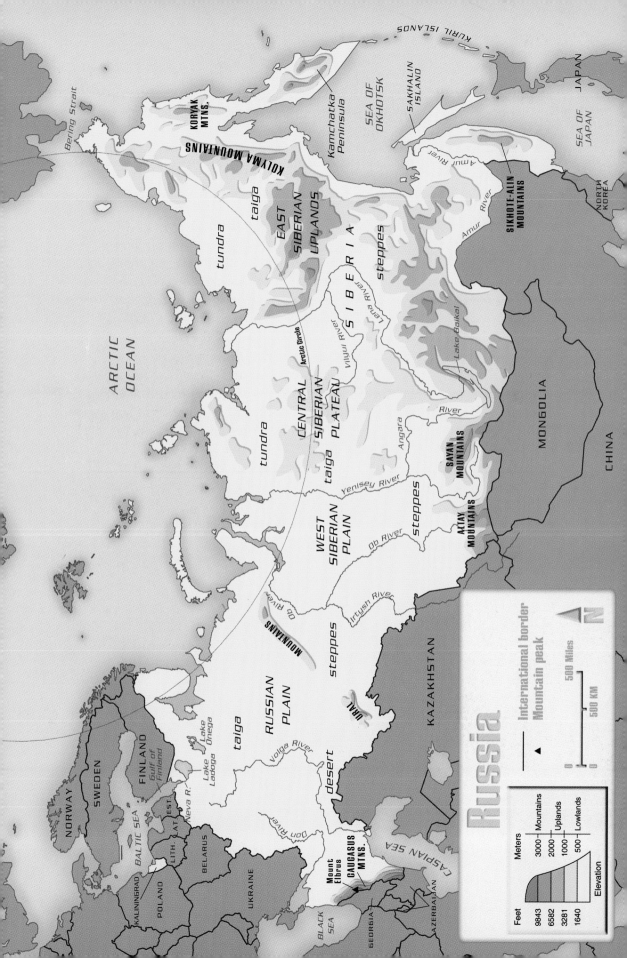

Russia

International border
▲ Mountain peak

N

	500 Miles
0	
0	500 KM

Feet	Meters	
9843	3000	Mountains
6582	2000	Uplands
3281	1000	
1640	500	Lowlands
		Elevation

ARCTIC OCEAN

Bering Strait

KORYAK MTNS.

KOLYMA MOUNTAINS

EAST SIBERIAN UPLANDS

Kamchatka Peninsula

SEA OF OKHOTSK

SAKHALIN ISLAND

KURIL ISLANDS

JAPAN

SEA OF JAPAN

NORTH KOREA

Amur River

SIKHOTE-ALIN MOUNTAINS

Amur River

tundra

taiga

SIBERIA

steppes

Lena River

Lake Baikal

Vilyui River

Arctic Circle

CENTRAL SIBERIAN PLATEAU

Angara River

River

SAYAN MOUNTAINS

MONGOLIA

CHINA

tundra

taiga

Yenisey River

steppes

ALTAY MOUNTAINS

WEST SIBERIAN PLAIN

Ob River

Irtysh River

KAZAKHSTAN

Ob River

MOUNTAINS

steppes

URAL

taiga

RUSSIAN PLAIN

Volga River

desert

CASPIAN SEA

Lake Onega

Lake Ladoga

Neva R.

Gulf of Finland

FINLAND

Don River

CAUCASUS MTNS.

Mount Elbrus

▲

GEORGIA

AZERBAIJAN

BLACK SEA

NORWAY

SWEDEN

BALTIC SEA

EST.

LAT.

LITH.

KALININGRAD

POLAND

BELARUS

UKRAINE

Russia is so large that it stretches across eleven time zones. Someone in the western part of the country might be having breakfast, while in the far eastern portion of the country another person is getting ready for bed.

PLATEAUS The West Siberian Plain gradually transforms into the Central Siberian Plateau, which begins east of the Yenisey River. The plateau is a sparsely populated area of about 1.5 million square miles (3.9 million sq. km) that is covered by forest, swamps, and arctic tundra. The plateau eventually reaches elevations of 2,000 feet (610 m) above sea level as it sweeps northeastward to meet mountains in the far east just past the Lena River.

MOUNTAINS The Ural Mountains provide one of the traditional borders between Europe and Asia. The Urals are relatively low, with most peaks rising to about 3,000 feet (914 m) above sea level and a few rising above 6,000 feet (1,829 m). East of the Lena River in Asia lie the East Siberian Uplands, which are filled

Frost covers the Vilyui River, which flows through the Central Siberian Plateau. Check out current weather conditions in Siberia and other parts of Russia at vgsbooks.com.

The Ural Mountains (the low green range in the background) cover about 2,500 miles (4,000 km) of western Russia.

with sparsely populated mountains reaching close to 10,000 feet (3,048 m) above sea level. The most spectacular part of the uplands is the Kamchatka Peninsula, which sits directly north of Japan. The peninsula includes many active volcanoes and geysers, along with rich stores of natural resources.

A series of mountain ranges also rises along Russia's southern border. The ranges begin in the southwest with the Caucasus Mountains, which lie between the Black and Caspian Seas. The Caucasus's dizzying heights include Mount Elbrus, the tallest mountain in Europe at 18,510 feet (5,642 m) above sea level. To the east, just north of China and Mongolia, are the Altay and Sayan Mountains. The Sayan are the start of a series of ranges to the south of the Central Siberian Plateau and eventually reach the Sikhote-Alin Mountains along the Sea of Japan. North of this range, on Russia's eastern coast, are the Kolyma Mountains. The Koryak Mountains extend northward along the Kamchatka Peninsula.

Rivers, Seas, and Lakes

Long before motorized transport, Russians traveled on the nation's 1.8 million miles (2.9 million km) of rivers. Although harsh winters freeze these waterways for months at a time, limiting their use to sleds on the ice, Russia's history remains tied to its rivers.

The Volga River—often called Mother Volga—is the country's principal waterway and Europe's longest river. It starts as a spring in hills north of Moscow and flows nearly 2,300 miles (3,701 km) southward to the Caspian Sea. On its way, the Volga crosses a huge wheat-growing region and flows through major cities such as Nizhniy Novgorod and Volgograd. The Don is another major river west of the Urals.

Although Russia's European rivers have been important to its development, the nation's longest river—the Ob, at 3,459 miles (5,567 km) long—is located in Asia. The Ob starts in the foothills of the Altay Mountains and travels northward across the West Siberian Plain to the

Arctic Ocean. Other rivers in Asian Russia are the Irtysh, the Yenisey, the Lena, and the Amur.

In addition to its rivers, Russia holds an estimated two million freshwater and saltwater seas and lakes. The most important of these is the Baltic Sea, which provides Russia with a short route to the Atlantic Ocean through the Gulf of Finland. Another important body of water is the Caspian Sea, which borders southern Russia. Covering an area of more than 140,000 square miles (362,600 sq. km), the Caspian is the largest inland saltwater sea in the world. However, the sea is shrinking, as it loses more water to evaporation than it gains from the rivers and streams that flow into it.

The largest lakes are Baikal, Ladoga, and Onega. Lake Baikal, located in southern Siberia near the Mongolian border, is the deepest freshwater lake in the world at about 5,700 feet (1,737 m) and contains approximately 20 percent of the earth's surface-level freshwater. The lake is 398 miles (640 km) long and covers about 12,200 square miles (31,598 sq. km). An estimated 336 rivers flow into the lake, but only one—the Angara—flows out.

BEAUTIFUL BAIKAL

Lake Baikal's water is among the purest in the world. The lake and its surroundings are home to about two thousand types of plants and animals, most of which are only found at Baikal. Among the regional animals are brown bears, elk, reindeer, moose, deer, and the *nerpa*—the only freshwater seal in the world. The lake is also famous for its fish, including salmon and sturgeon.

Long, fingerlike freshwater sponges float in the pristine waters of Siberia's **Lake Baikal.**

Climate

Many people picture bitter Siberian winters when they think of Russia. But the country is so large that it has a wide variety of climates. Temperatures range from well below freezing to near 100°F (38°C).

European Russia has long winters and short, dry summers, and Moscow experiences average temperatures of 15°F (–9°C) in winter and 66°F (19°C) in summer. Truly cold weather hits the region eastward across the Urals and into the Arctic Circle, where fierce blizzards blow throughout much of the winter and the land lies under a blanket of snow most of the year. Some of the coldest spots in the world are located in eastern Siberia, where temperatures can drop as low as –95°F (–71°C). Novosibirsk, Siberia's largest city, has an average winter temperature of –15°F (–26°C). However, Siberia can get warm in the summers. Novosibirsk averages 75°F (24°C) in summer, while the south central areas of Asian Russia have been known to register temperatures as high as 120°F (49°C) in the summer.

The most moderate temperatures are found in the southwestern region, especially along the coasts. Winter temperatures usually remain above 30°F (–1°C), while summer averages are above 80°F (27°C).

Russia gets a lot of moisture during the year. In European Russia, as much as 100 inches (254 centimeters) fall each year, with Moscow getting between 20 and 30 inches (51 and 76 cm) of rain annually. In chilly central and eastern Russia, most of the moisture falls as snow.

Permafrost is a condition in which the ground remains frozen year-round. Permafrost covers about half of all the land in Russia, and in northern Siberia the permafrost goes as deep as 5,000 feet (1,524 m). The Siberian town of Verkhoyansk is considered the coldest settled place on earth. It has also registered the greatest known temperature swings, recording a high temperature of 98°F (37°C) and a low of –90°F (–69°C).

Flora and Fauna

Each of Russia's distinct vegetation zones has its own unique flora, with weather playing a great role in the variety. The tundra has no forests, but a few hardy bushes, small trees, and mosses weather the cold. Although the deep ground remains frozen, snow and ice on the surface melt into mosquito-filled marshes in the summer.

South of the tundra, the large swath of taiga includes fir, pine, cedar, aspen, oak, maple, poplar, birch, and ash trees. Still farther south, the

RUSSIAN RARITIES

Some of the rarest and most beautiful big cats on earth are found in Siberia. The Siberian tiger is larger than tigers in India. Its heavier fur keeps it warm during the long Russian winter. The Amur leopard *(below)*, another rare cat, can run at a speed of 37 miles per hour (60 km per hour) and can jump 20 feet (6 m) horizontally and 10 feet (3 m) vertically. Only about 350 Siberian tigers and 40 Amur leopards remain in the world, and Russia has established conservation programs to protect these native creatures.

grassy steppes are dotted with flowers. The coastal Black Sea's climate is perfect for lush magnolia, eucalyptus, and hibiscus trees.

The thousands of animal species that roam Russia are as varied as the country's geography and climate. Polar bears and reindeer are found in the tundra, along with foxes and lemmings. The forests are home to Russia's national symbol, the brown bear, as well as hares, mink, sables, wolves, and deer. Rare Siberian tigers and Amur leopards are found in the remote eastern taiga, while the steppes contain smaller animals, such as mice and hamsters. The desert regions of southwestern Russia contain snakes, lizards, antelope, and gazelles, and western coastal areas hold wild boars and porcupines.

Natural Resources and Environmental Challenges

Russia contains a wide array of natural resources, including major deposits of oil, natural gas, coal, and nickel. Russian mineral resources are found all over the country, but Siberia holds the nation's most lucrative deposits of oil and gas. The land also yields smaller amounts of many valuable minerals, such as gold, diamonds, platinum, silver, lead, copper, and tin. However, a major problem facing Russia is that so much of the country is covered by permanently frozen ground that getting to the minerals can be very difficult and expensive.

Siberian coal mine

Timber is also one of Russia's greatest resources. The nation has more forested land than any country in the world. The World Bank estimates that more than 3 million square miles (7.7 million sq. km) of forest area lie within Russia, most of which are in the remote Siberian wilderness.

The nation's long coastline and rivers provide valuable harvests of fish and seafood. The Russian fishing industry is one of the world's largest, and Russia is one of the leading producers of frozen and canned fish.

But many of Russia's natural resources are in danger. Deforestation is a great concern, as the land's vast forests are harvested at a high rate. In addition, years of industrialization have had a terrible environmental impact, especially on the country's waterways. Chemicals from large industries and the illegal dumping of industrial waste have polluted rivers and lakes. The search for oil in Siberia has led to numerous spills that have contaminated waterways with crude oil. The country has also faced dangerous nuclear accidents and nuclear waste hazards. The worst accident took place in 1986, when an explosion occurred at the Chernobyl nuclear power plant (part of modern Ukraine). Radiation escaped the plant, requiring more than 100,000 people to be evacuated from the surrounding area. In addition, thousands of cleanup workers were estimated to have been killed or made ill by the radiation. Russians hope that the country's leaders will pay greater attention to conservation and environmental safety in the future.

Cities

Although sparsely populated overall, Russia is primarily an urban country, with about 73 percent of the population living in cities. The most important cities include Moscow, Saint Petersburg, and Novosibirsk.

MOSCOW Located on the banks of the Moscow River, Moscow is the nation's capital and home to about 9 million people. The city was first

Pedestrians stroll through **Menage Square in Moscow.** Moscow is the most recent in a long list of cities to serve as Russia's capital.

mentioned in history books in 1147 and became the main force in uniting Russia and turning it into an empire. The city grew around a fortress called the Kremlin, where the modern federal government is housed. The Kremlin is located at Red Square, which also holds Lenin's tomb, Saint Basil's Cathedral, and GUM—a shopping mall that was formerly one of the world's biggest department stores. Moscow continues to have major cultural importance, especially as the spiritual center of the Russian Orthodox Church. The city is also a manufacturing hub with many factories.

SAINT PETERSBURG With a population of almost 5 million, Saint Petersburg is Russia's second largest city. Located on the banks of the Neva River along the Gulf of Finland, the city was built by Czar Peter the Great in 1703. It is often called "the Venice of the North" because of its many canals and its European architecture. (Venice is a city built on a lagoon in northern Italy.) Saint Petersburg became Russia's capital in 1712. In 1914, when Russia fought Germany in World War I, Czar Nicholas II renamed the city Petrograd to make the name sound less German. The name changed again in 1924 when the Communists named the city Leningrad after Lenin, and in 1991 Saint Petersburg

finally regained its original name. The city's attractions include the Hermitage Museum, the Winter Palace (the former home of the czars), and the Peter and Paul Fortress.

NOVOSIBIRSK Often called the capital of Siberia, Novosibirsk is the third largest city in Russia with close to 1.5 million people. The city lies on the banks of the Ob River and was founded in 1893 during the construction of the Trans-Siberian Railroad. The city is still one of the most important stops on the railroad, and it remains a hub of industry and transportation. The city is also considered Siberia's primary cultural center, with the region's largest art gallery, a world-class opera and ballet company, a famous symphony, and jazz groups of renown. Since the opening of a large branch of the Academy of Sciences in the 1950s, Novosibirsk has also been a major research center.

Visit vgsbooks.com for links where you can learn more about what there is to see and do in Moscow and Saint Petersburg. Find a direct link to the Hermitage Museum and more.

HISTORY AND GOVERNMENT

Humans have lived on the plains of Russia and eastern Europe for thousands of years, but it was not until about the seventh or eighth century that the people who became Russians dominated the area. A group called the Eastern Slavs, who were originally part of a larger Slavic group, eventually established settlements in what would become European Russia.

◉ Kievan Rus

The towns founded by the Eastern Slavs—including Novgorod (in western Russia) and Kiev (in Ukraine)—benefited from their locations along important trade routes between Scandinavia in the north and the Byzantine Empire in the south. But the wealth of the area soon attracted raiders from Scandinavia called Varangians—better known as Vikings—who conquered the Eastern Slav villages.

The most successful Varangian invader, Rurik, conquered Novgorod in 862. Rurik's successor, Oleg, captured Kiev in 882 and went on to establish a state called Kievan Rus.

In 988 Vladimir, a successor of Oleg, joined the Greek Orthodox Church and made Christianity the state religion of Kievan Rus. This event was an important turning point in Russian history, as it also marked the creation of the Russian Orthodox Church.

The Mongol Yoke

Although Kievan Rus prospered, its princes often fought among themselves for control. During the eleventh and twelfth centuries, this internal conflict left the state vulnerable to outside enemies. By the 1200s, an army of skilled Asian horsemen and fighters called the Mongols had swept into Russia. Led by Genghis Khan and later by his grandson Batu Khan, the Mongols seized and destroyed scores of Russian cities. By 1240 Russia had become part of the Mongol Empire.

The Mongols allowed local rulers to stay in power, provided that they paid tribute (taxes) and supplied soldiers to the Mongol army. Although they permitted limited freedoms, the Mongols greatly influenced

This artwork depicts **a Russian army about to battle the Mongols in 1380.** Dmitri Donskoi, the group's leader, is being blessed by a priest. Although the Russians won this battle, it took them another one hundred years to drive out the Mongols.

Russian language, culture, and dress. One great beneficiary of Mongol rule was Muscovy, a principality (an area controlled by a prince) strategically located on a prime trade route. Muscovy, later called Moscow, soon grew to rival Novgorod and Kiev. By the early fourteenth century, Moscow had become the strongest principality in Russia, and the Russian Orthodox Church had moved its headquarters there from Kiev. Meanwhile, the Mongol hold on Russia began to weaken. It was finally broken by the grand duke of Moscow, Ivan III, who refused to pay further tribute to the Mongols in 1480.

The Czars

Ivan III (also called Ivan the Great) took power and built Moscow into one of the great cities of the world and took over the principalities of Tver and Novgorod. He was also the first ruler to consider himself emperor, or czar, of Russia. His reign, which lasted until 1505, laid the foundation of the Russian Empire.

Ivan IV, Ivan the Great's grandson, became czar in 1533, at age three, although his mother acted as ruler until he was seventeen years old. Ivan IV enjoyed great military success and expanded the Russian Empire southward to the Caspian Sea and eastward across the Ural Mountains to Siberia. To celebrate his successes, he had the magnificent Saint Basil's Cathedral built in Moscow.

But Ivan IV eventually came to be known as Ivan the Terrible because of his ugly temper and bloody actions. He is believed to have killed his favorite son in a fit of rage, and he constantly fought against his own people. He battled aristocratic landowners, called boyars, who sought more land and power. He created a national assembly, which he controlled, called the *zemsky sobor*. He also created the *oprichniki*, a secret police force, to take over the estates of the boyars. The oprichniki also was used to control the Russian peasants. An unofficial system employed these farm laborers to work and live on Russian estates, often under harsh conditions. Called serfs, these workers had limited rights. For example, the oprichniki helped enforce a rule that serfs could not leave the lands they worked.

Ivan the Terrible died in 1584, rumored to have been poisoned by political rivals. Whatever the cause of his death, it only plunged Russia into deeper problems. Ivan's son, Fyodor, took over the throne but proved to be a poor ruler. Fyodor's brother-in-law, Boris Godunov, actually ran the government from behind the scenes. When Fyodor died and his brother Dmitri was believed to have been murdered, no heir stood in line for the throne. Godunov took

RISE OF THE COSSACKS

During Ivan the Terrible's reign, many serfs escaped from their estates and set up their own communities. These serfs eventually formed an army known as the Cossacks, meaning horseman or freeman, and became famous worldwide as ferocious soldiers and great horsemen. Cossacks were virtually independent except for military service, which they were required to provide to the Russian government.

A Cossack makes his way into battle. The Cossacks organized themselves into groups by location. Cossack communities elected *hetmans* as their leaders.

over in 1598, and his reign—known as the "Time of Troubles"—was characterized by violence, unrest, and crushing famine.

The Romanov Dynasty

The Time of Troubles ended at last in 1613, when the zemsky sobor chose Mikhail Romanov as the new czar. The first ruler of the Romanov dynasty (family of rulers), Mikhail Romanov was the grandnephew of Ivan the Terrible. A teenager when he assumed power, the young czar greatly expanded Russia's territory to the east, reaching deep into Siberia. One expedition even reached the Pacific Coast.

But some of the policies instituted by the first Romanov and his successors eventually led to unrest. In 1649 serfdom became a legal institution, all but imprisoning the peasants. Many serfs fled the estates to which they were bound. Others organized a large revolt in 1670. Russian troops defeated the rebels, but the expenses of dealing with uprisings and paying for a growing government bureaucracy were constant drains on the national treasury.

In 1682 two half-brothers, Peter I and Ivan V, shared the crown. When Ivan died in 1696, Peter, a great-grandson of Mikhail Romanov, assumed absolute power.

Peter, who became known as Peter the Great, traveled throughout Europe, often in disguise. Impressed at the progress the continent was

Peter the Great

making, he decided to modernize Russia using European methods. He restructured the army and created the navy. He drafted peasants as soldiers, appointed nobles as officers, and provided all members of the army and navy with military training. This military overhaul encouraged the foundation of many factories to produce weapons. More factories soon sprang up in Russia, producing textiles and other goods and creating thousands of jobs in industry.

Peter also brought the Russian Orthodox Church under the government's control, reformed government ministries, and made education mandatory for children of the country's nobles. To mark the start of a new Russia, he created a great new city in 1703. He called it Saint Petersburg and in 1712 made it the capital of Russia.

A succession of rulers followed Peter the Great's death in 1725. Peter III, one of these successors, was assassinated in 1762. His German wife, Catherine II, assumed the throne as czarina, or empress.

Peter III and Catherine II pose for a portrait.

Many people believed that Catherine, deeply ambitious, had been part of the plot to kill her husband. After taking power, Catherine, who came to be known as Catherine the Great, continued to expand Russia. During her reign, the Russian Empire stretched from the Baltic Sea to the Pacific Ocean.

Catherine's reign was also noted for great cultural growth. The empress was interested in literature, science, and art. She exchanged letters and ideas with some of the greatest thinkers in the world. She also encouraged education for women in Russia.

But, like other Russian rulers, Catherine dealt harshly with the serfs. Peasant uprisings, especially one in European Russia in 1773, gave her the chance to further concentrate power in her hands and in the hands of the nation's landholders. Her policies further widened the gap

A group of peasants rallies around its leader during the **revolt of 1773.** Rebel leader Yemelyan Pugachov *(seated on horse)* was a Cossack.

between the rich and the poor, as Russia's aristocracy grew even wealthier and more privileged, while the serfs remained nearly destitute.

The 1800s

Russian expansion drew the attention of European countries, such as France, then one of the world's most powerful nations. In June 1812, the French general Napoleon Bonaparte, eager to seize some of Russia's riches for himself, led six hundred thousand troops into Russia. The French advanced quickly toward Moscow. Facing a superior army, the Russians retreated. But Moscow burned behind them, and some historians believe that the Russians burned their own cities and fields to deprive the French army of food and shelter.

The "scorched earth" policy also bought Russia time as winter approached. The harsh conditions forced Napoleon to retreat. As the French moved westward, the Russians kept attacking, slowly reducing the size of Napoleon's army until it was beaten. This great victory confirmed Russia as a major European power.

Despite its rise to prominence, Russia still struggled with turmoil. New ideas of freedom, liberty, and equality were spreading in Europe and began to take hold in Russia. Underground groups formed with the goals of limiting the czar's power and of abolishing serfdom.

In December 1825, shortly after Czar Nicholas I took power, a group of rebels called the Decembrists struck. They hoped to spark a revolution that would topple the monarchy and lead to a more democratic form of government. But the uprising met a quick end when the new czar's armed guards fired on the protesters with cannons. Nicholas, meanwhile, also faced international conflicts. In 1854, for

The Decembrists were able to fire a few shots from their gathering place at Senate Square in Saint Petersburg before being dispersed by the czar's cannons.

Russian troops charge into Battle at Balaklava during the Crimean War.

example, the czar's troops fought in the Crimean War against the Ottoman Empire (an empire comprising modern Turkey and other nations). The war arose over land disputes, especially concerning holy sites in areas controlled by the Ottomans. Shortly after Nicholas died in 1855, the war ended in a humiliating defeat for Russia.

When Alexander II succeeded that same year, he tried to heal his country's wounds. He loosened government control at the local level, improved the legal and educational systems, and reorganized the army. Between 1858 and 1860, he expanded Siberia's territory along the Pacific coast.

Alexander II

One of Alexander's most historic acts—which earned him the name "Alexander the Liberator"— was the abolishment of serfdom in 1861. However, the new law did not immediately free anyone, as serfs had to buy their liberty. Few of the poverty-stricken peasants could afford the payments, and they deeply resented the requirement. The change also upset the landowners, whose wealth depended on the cheap labor of the serfs.

Numerous demonstrations resulted, and the government cracked down with restrictive measures including censorship. In 1881 a terrorist killed Alexander II in Saint Petersburg, and Alexander III took over. He imposed further limits on the press and tightened control over local governments. He also gave landholders more power, further fueling the growing anger of the poor.

The Last Czar

Alexander III died in 1894, and his son Nicholas ascended the throne at the age of twenty-six. Czar Nicholas II took over a Russia flourishing in literature, art, dance, and music. But the growth in culture masked great turmoil in Russian society. Antigovernment sentiment kept growing, rebels grew bolder, and new groups formed to oppose the monarchy.

Among these groups were the Marxists, who were followers of the ideals of the nineteenth-century German economist Karl Marx. Marx believed that history was determined by the economic struggle between the rich and the poor, the bosses and the workers. He predicted that workers would eventually rebel and take over the government, creating a workers' paradise. His ideas caught hold in Russia, where masses of poor peasants and factory workers struggled to survive, while the aristocracy attended glittering parties and balls.

Russian Marxists formed the Russian Social Democratic Labor Party. Internal disputes led the group to split into the Bolsheviks and the Mensheviks. Among the Bolsheviks was an ambitious young Marxist named Vladimir Ilich Lenin, who aspired to create the idyllic workers' state envisioned by Marx.

Vladimir Ilich Lenin

Nicholas had little experience, and he was unprepared to deal with the increasingly organized opposition to his control. He was also easily led by his advisers, who in 1904 convinced him to fight a war against Japan over disputed territory. The Russo-Japanese War ended in an embarrassing and costly defeat for Russia, and dissatisfaction with the young czar grew.

On Sunday, January 22, 1905, a group of workers led by a Russian Orthodox priest, Father George Gapon, marched to the czar's palace in Saint Petersburg to demand changes. The czar's guards reacted with violence, killing more than 130 protesters and wounding hundreds more. Riots and strikes broke out across the country

Father George Gapon *(at center, in black robe)* **led workers in a 1905 protest in Saint Petersburg. The march ended in such violence that it earned the name "Bloody Sunday."**

following "Bloody Sunday." The threat of full-scale revolution forced Nicholas to sign the October Manifesto, which established a constitution and introduced limited democratic reforms, including the formation of a legislature called the Duma. Duma representatives, who advised the czar and approved laws, were appointed by local councils elected by men in each region. (Women were not yet allowed to vote.)

World War I and the October Revolution

While embroiled in these internal troubles, the nation was soon drawn into international conflict. When World War I broke out in 1914, Russia joined Great Britain and France in the war against Germany. The war quickly grew unpopular at home, as the Russian army suffered defeats at the hands of the better-prepared and better-supplied Germans.

Nicholas's troubles grew with the presence of Grigory Rasputin, a Siberian peasant who claimed to have mystical healing powers. Rasputin convinced Empress Alexandra, the czar's wife, that he could ease her son Alexis's hemophilia, a life-threatening blood disease. Because young Alexis was the czarevitch—the heir to the Romanov throne—his health was of the utmost importance to the family and the empire. Through his power over Alexandra, Rasputin also exercised an influence on the government. Members of the Russian aristocracy, believing that Rasputin was a threat to both the nation and to the imperial family, killed him in 1916.

Grigory Rasputin

Meanwhile, the war dragged on. The Russian army and people were running short of food, fuel, and shelter, and soldiers began deserting by the thousands. In March 1917, rioting broke out in Moscow and Saint Petersburg. The nation's stability was swiftly collapsing. Nicholas ordered Russian troops to stop the rioters and restore order. But, instead, the czar's soldiers joined the rebels. Faced with this final challenge, Nicholas saw no choice but to give up his throne.

Late on the night of November 6, 1917, the Russian Revolution—also called the October Revolution—began. The Bolshevik Party, led by Lenin, took over the government and established the Russian Soviet Federative Socialist Republic. The new government, based on Communist principles influenced by Marxism, was the first of its kind.

The basic ideas of Communism, similar to those of Marxism, are that society's problems are caused by conflict between social classes. Peace and happiness, according to Communism, can be achieved by

The people who fought in the **Russian Revolution** came from many backgrounds. Many were peasants. Others were factory workers. Still others were ex-soldiers from the czar's army.

creating a nation without classes or private property. In this type of state, the government owns all property and makes decisions based upon what is good for the people as a whole, not just for one person or for certain groups of people.

Renaming his political group the Communist Party, Lenin moved Russia's capital back to Moscow and removed the country from World War I in March 1918. In the summer of 1918, Lenin ordered the execution of the royal family, which had been under arrest since the October Revolution. Russian soldiers shot Nicholas, Alexandra, and all five of their children and threw their bodies into wells in a nearby forest.

To gain full control of Russia, Lenin's troops, called the Workers' and Peasants' Red Army, had to fight the White Russians, anti-Communists who were trying to overthrow Lenin's government. The ensuing civil war ended with the Bolsheviks' victory in 1920, but it left the country in serious economic trouble. Lenin tried to ease the situation by nationalizing (transferring to state control) all industries and agricultural production. Problems multiplied when a drought in 1920 and 1921 caused a famine that killed five million people. In response, Lenin issued his New Economic Policy, which returned some businesses to private control and

THE MYSTERY PRINCESS

The fate of Anastasia, Czar Nicholas II's youngest daughter, has been a source of rumors and gossip for almost one hundred years. After the revolutionaries executed the Romanov family, rumors spread almost immediately that Anastasia had somehow escaped. A woman named Anna Anderson was among many who came forward to claim Anastasia's identity. Anderson appeared in Berlin in 1920 and raised quite a stir, but DNA evidence later determined that Anderson was not a family member.

allowed farmers to keep some of their harvests. The policies helped, but Russia's troubles were too big to fix so easily.

● The Soviet Union, Stalin, and World War II

Seeking to expand Communism to other countries, Lenin took over the ruling councils, or soviets, of neighboring republics such as Ukraine, Belarus, Azerbaijan, Georgia, and Armenia. In 1922 Lenin unified this group of republics into the Union of Soviet Socialist Republics, also called the Soviet Union or USSR.

After Lenin's death in 1924, Joseph Stalin became the leader of the Communist Party, which held most of the government's power. During his reign, Stalin tried to portray himself as an all-powerful, godlike figure. He took absolute control of nearly every aspect of Soviet life. He dictated where people lived, who held political office, which movies were made, what books and newspapers were published, and what education Soviet children received.

One of Stalin's early acts was to replace Lenin's New Economic Policy with the first Five-Year Plan, which outlined production goals that Soviet industry and agriculture were supposed to achieve. In the 1930s, Stalin pushed toward these goals by forcing millions of people to work on collective farms. At these large agricultural complexes, many families lived and worked together. Farmers were required to turn over virtually all of their harvests to the government to meet

During his rise to power as leader of the Soviet Union, **Joseph Stalin** eliminated his political opponents.

rigorous production quotas. The system resulted in a crushing famine that killed millions between 1932 and 1933.

Stalin also imprisoned and killed millions of people whom he saw as political threats. These devastating purges came to be known as the Great Terror. Among the people Stalin targeted were scientists, politicians, military officers, labor leaders, and workers. To contain his prisoners, Stalin created gulags—a vast system of labor camps and prisons in Siberia and around the country. Many people were sent to the gulags after trials in which they were forced to confess to crimes that they had not committed. Frequent arrests, strict censorship, and harsh punishments led many citizens to feel afraid of their own government and suspicious of their own neighbors. Stalin also persecuted Russia's national minorities—ethnic groups that lived within Russia and the Soviet Union's republics.

Stalin's desire for power was soon threatened by Germany. Under the leadership of the Nazi Party and Adolf Hitler, Germany was seizing large amounts of land in central and eastern Europe. To protect Russia, Stalin signed an alliance with Hitler in 1939. The pact stated that the two countries would not invade one another but that each would attempt to seize other eastern European nations. Following the pact, Stalin annexed (took over) the Baltic States of Latvia, Lithuania, and Estonia.

But World War II began soon after the signing of the treaty, and within two years Hitler had betrayed Stalin. Hungry for more land and eager to crush the USSR's Communist government, Hitler ordered Nazi troops into the Soviet Union on June 22, 1941. Forced by the invasion to enter the war, which Russians came to call the Great Patriotic War, the Soviet Union joined on the side of the Allies with the United States and Britain.

The German army soon held much of the European areas of the Soviet Union. Within six months, German soldiers had surrounded Leningrad (formerly Saint Petersburg), and German artillery pounded the city during the twenty-nine-month siege that followed. Food ran short, and more than one million people died during the battle before the Germans were finally pushed back. But German victories continued as Nazi troops moved toward Moscow.

By 1943 the Germans had besieged the city of Stalingrad (later renamed Volgograd). But they met fierce resistance. Although the Germans virtually destroyed the city, the Battle of Stalingrad decimated the Nazi ranks, eventually allowing USSR forces to achieve the surrender of more than three hundred thousand German troops.

After the victory at Stalingrad, Stalin's troops pushed through eastern Europe toward the heart of Germany. On May 2, 1945, the Soviet army marched into Berlin, Germany's capital. Within a week, Germany had surrendered.

After defeating German troops in Berlin, **soldiers raise the Soviet flag** over a German government building. USSR forces were key in defeating the Nazis during World War II.

The Cold War

Germany's surrender did not mark the end of the war. Britain and the United States were also fighting Japan. The Soviet Union turned to help its allies, declaring war on Japan on August 8, 1945. Japan surrendered on September 2, 1945. Although the Soviet Union was on the winning side of the war, it lost more than twenty million soldiers and civilians to the conflict.

After the war, the Allies began carving up the captured lands. The USSR gained the Kuril Islands and part of Sakhalin Island from Japan. The USSR also took parts of Poland and Czechoslovakia. In addition, Soviet-supported Communist parties took power in Poland, Hungary, Romania, Bulgaria, Czechoslovakia, and East Germany (which was created after Nazi Germany was divided into two countries). Stalin had achieved his ambition of making the Soviet Union one of the most powerful countries in the world. So much of eastern Europe was controlled by the Soviet Union and Communists that British prime minister Winston Churchill declared that an "Iron Curtain" had fallen between eastern and western Europe.

The United States, suspicious of the Communist system, soon became a bitter rival of the Soviet Union. Tensions rose in 1949 when China, the world's most populous country, became Communist. Around the same time, the Soviet Union began building nuclear bombs, becoming the only nation other than the United States to have such weapons. The mounting rivalry produced the Cold War, a conflict that never escalated into an armed war but that pitted the Soviet Union against the United States in a contest to see whose political system would prevail.

KHRUSHCHEV After Stalin's death in 1953, Nikita Khrushchev took over as leader of the Communist Party. Although Khrushchev had been a close ally of Stalin's, he loosened many harsh policies. This "de-Stalinization" included allowing the Soviet Union to coexist peacefully with non-Communist nations.

Nikita Khrushchev

Khrushchev, however, continued the Cold War, funding costly programs to make his country better than the United States. The two nations engaged in the arms race, in which each side tried to create bigger armies and more nuclear weapons. Khrushchev also boosted the country's science programs, sparking what came to be called the space race, as the

The Russian satellite *Sputnik I* had two radio transmitters that broadcast a "beep-beep-beep" sound. Although this may seem like a tiny accomplishment in the twenty-first century, *Sputnik I* ushered in the space age.

USSR and the United States raced to be the first with satellites and astronauts in space.

Although Khrushchev's government preached peaceful coexistence, he did bring his country into confrontations with the United States. The two nations came to the brink of war during the Cuban Missile Crisis of 1962. The United States had missiles in Europe and Asia pointing at the Soviet Union. When Khrushchev placed similar missiles in Cuba, 90 miles (145 km) from the United States, the act drew an angry response from President John F. Kennedy, who ordered U.S. forces to block Soviet ships on their way to Cuba. The world watched anxiously, fearing that a devastating nuclear war would break out between the two superpowers. After about a week, the crisis ended when Khrushchev ordered the Soviet ships to return home. But this was also the beginning of the end for Khrushchev. Low harvests, low industrial production, and a lack of support for reform led to Khrushchev's being replaced in 1964.

SPACE RACE

The Soviets won the first lap of the space race when they launched *Sputnik I* on October 4, 1957. Sputnik stayed in space until early 1958, orbiting Earth every 96 minutes. The Russians also sent the first human being into space, launching cosmonaut (Soviet astronaut) Yury Gagarin into orbit aboard *Vostok I* on April 12, 1961. The first woman in space was also a Russian, Valentina Tereshkova, who went into space on *Vostok IV* in 1963.

THE BREZHNEV ERA Leonid Brezhnev followed Khrushchev as the head of the Communist Party. Brezhnev reinstituted some severe policies, limiting the activities of human-rights supporters and taking many freedoms away from the Soviet Union's national minorities. He also created the Brezhnev Doctrine, which stated that the Soviet Union would send troops to help "friendly" governments in eastern Europe if it appeared that they were unstable. Brezhnev used this policy to spread and protect Communism and to keep Communist governments loyal to the USSR. For example, he sent Soviet troops into Czechoslovakia in 1968, when Communist leaders there tried to loosen Moscow's hold.

Brezhnev also continued the Cold War, as the Soviet Union and the United States supported opposing sides in wars in the Middle East, in Central America, and in Africa. But the rivalry proved costly to the Soviet Union, which could hardly afford to produce enough food or quality products for its people. In the early 1970s, Brezhnev invited U.S. president Richard Nixon to Moscow to discuss détente, the easing of tensions between the two countries. In 1972 the two countries made a great step forward by signing the Strategic Arms Limitation Talks (SALT) to reduce nuclear weapons.

Improved international relations, however, did little to improve the Soviet Union's situation. Poor harvests forced the country to import grain during the 1970s. The national government continued to be inefficient. Long lines and shortages of food and fuel were a constant part of Soviet life. And late in 1979, Brezhnev sent Soviet troops into Afghanistan to support a struggling Communist government there. Many countries were outraged by what they saw as an aggressive invasion of a much smaller country.

If you'd like to find out more about Russia's complex history, go to vgsbooks.com where you'll find links to information on Communism, the Cold War, and much more.

 ## A New Russia

By the time Brezhnev died in 1982, his country was ready for new leadership. In 1985, after a series of short-lived successors, Mikhail Gorbachev took over, and the country took a new turn. Gorbachev moved to reform the government and the Communist Party through glasnost (openness) and perestroika (restructuring). He hoped to expand people's freedoms and to require more government accountability, while still keeping the Communists in power.

Gorbachev's ideas took hold so quickly and so thoroughly that the open discussion of ideas led many people to voice their anger and to question the wisdom of Communist rule. This questioning of authority was especially loud in the smaller republics of the USSR. Lands such as Armenia, Kazakhstan, Ukraine, Georgia, and the Baltic States sought independence from Moscow. At the same time, people in Communist

Mikhail Gorbachev *(right)* shakes hands with U.S. president George H. W. Bush at a press conference in Moscow. Gorbachev's government made efforts to end the Cold War and to create a good relationship with the United States.

countries such as Romania and East Germany rose up against their governments. In 1989, just after the long-awaited end of the ten-year Afghan war, the Berlin Wall came down. The wall, which had cut Berlin in two since Germany's division after World War II, had been a powerful symbol of Communism. Its collapse created a wave of anti-Communist feeling, resulting in the overthrow of numerous Communist governments under Soviet influence. The wave washed over the Soviet Union at the beginning of the 1990s. Gorbachev struggled to keep his country together, but he could not save the Soviet Union. Opposition to his rule—spearheaded by Boris Yeltsin, the leader of the Russian Republic's legislature—strengthened. Gorbachev resigned on December 25, 1991. On December 26, 1991, Yeltsin and his supporters declared the USSR formally dissolved.

As the Soviet Union ended, some republics joined Russia to form the Russian Federation, with Boris Yeltsin as president. Yeltsin's government also signed treaties with many of the republics that had once tried to gain independence from the USSR, creating a loose alliance called the Commonwealth of Independent States. Each country remained independent but promised to cooperate on trade and other matters.

Russia's transformation did not happen easily. Yeltsin fought with the legislature over how to reshape the country. In October 1993, the conflict turned violent. Opponents to Yeltsin seized several government buildings, and Yeltsin ordered the army to attack. The fighting led to numerous deaths, but Yeltsin was victorious. In 1994 Yeltsin faced a new conflict as the Republic of Chechnya tried to separate from Russia. Russia responded with military force, killing thousands of Chechens. But the Chechens were tough fighters, and their tactics took a heavy toll on Russian troops. In 1996 Russian troops withdrew. The two sides negotiated a peace treaty, but peace remained fragile.

Ongoing Struggles

The turmoil of the 1990s culminated in a deep financial crisis, and Yeltsin, who had developed health problems, left office at the end of 1999. Vladimir Putin stepped in as acting president and was officially elected in March 2000. In the early 2000s, Putin made efforts to further fortify Russia's relationship with outside nations. He also introduced reforms improving Russia's economy, strengthening democracy, and allowing greater freedom of expression. But Putin met strong resistance from conservatives who hoped that Russia would one day regain its superpower status.

Problems also resurfaced in Chechnya, where skirmishes between Russians and Chechens had dissolved the peace treaty. Russian forces had returned to the republic in late 1999, and the resulting fighting inflicted heavy casualties on both sides. Fighting still raged in 2002, and in October of that year, Chechen terrorists seized a Moscow theater, demanding the republic's independence and an end to the war. However, the conflict in Chechnya shows no signs of lessening.

In early 2003, Russia found itself at odds once again with the United States and other nations. Members of the international community debated the issue of a potential war against Iraq over its possession of nuclear and chemical weapons. While U.S. and British leaders supported the war, Russia threatened to veto any pro-war decisions in the United Nations.

TERROR AND TRAGEDY

The Chechen terror attack in Moscow ended after a fifty-eight-hour standoff. Russian troops rescued more than seven hundred hostages by using gas to knock out the terrorists. But the price was high. More than one hundred hostages died after inhaling the toxic gas, and hundreds of others were hospitalized. About fifty of the Chechen rebels were also killed by the gas and by gunfire from Russian troops. Meanwhile, many civilians in both Russia and Chechnya still long for a peaceful end to the Chechen conflict.

Government

The government of the Russian Federation is made up of executive, legislative, and judicial branches. The executive branch, based on a constitution, is headed by a president who is elected to a four-year term, acts as chief of state, and appoints a prime minister, agency heads, and other officials.

Russia's legislative branch of government, **the State Duma,** meets in these chambers in Moscow.

The legislative branch consists of two chambers, the Federation Council and the State Duma, which together make up the Federal Assembly. The judicial branch consists of the Constitutional Court, the Supreme Court, and the Supreme Arbitration Court.

Although the Communist Party was once the only recognized political party in the country, more than 150 political parties exist in present-day Russia, with more than a dozen of them represented in the Duma. However, Russia still has a strong Communist presence— approximately one-quarter of the seats in the Duma are filled by Communist Party members.

Russia is divided into many units for administration. It consists of twenty-one republics; forty-nine administrative regions, or oblasts; ten autonomous areas, or *okrugs;* six provinces, or *krays;* two federal cities; and one autonomous region.

THE PEOPLE

Russia—the largest country in the world—is shrinking, at least in terms of population. In 2002 the country had an estimated population of 143.5 million. But that number is falling. Only 9 births take place for every 16 deaths, and it is estimated that by 2025 Russia will have 129.1 million people. By 2050 the population could drop to 101.7 million.

With fewer and fewer people to fill its vast spaces, Russia is sparsely populated. There are about 22 people per square mile (57 per sq. km), compared to 207 people per square mile (536 per sq. km) in the former Soviet republic of Ukraine and 77 people per square mile (199 per sq. km) in the United States. Nevertheless, Russia has more than one thousand major cities, including at least a dozen with 1 million people or more. The population centers tend to be concentrated near rivers and lakes, and the vast majority of the population—about 73 percent—lives in urban areas, primarily in cities west of the Ural Mountains.

web enhanced @ www.vgsbooks.com

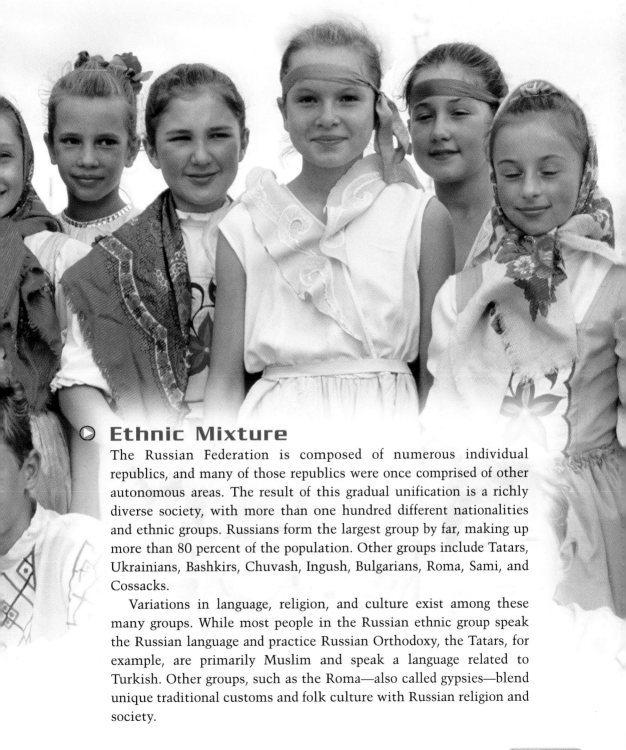

◉ Ethnic Mixture

The Russian Federation is composed of numerous individual republics, and many of those republics were once comprised of other autonomous areas. The result of this gradual unification is a richly diverse society, with more than one hundred different nationalities and ethnic groups. Russians form the largest group by far, making up more than 80 percent of the population. Other groups include Tatars, Ukrainians, Bashkirs, Chuvash, Ingush, Bulgarians, Roma, Sami, and Cossacks.

Variations in language, religion, and culture exist among these many groups. While most people in the Russian ethnic group speak the Russian language and practice Russian Orthodoxy, the Tatars, for example, are primarily Muslim and speak a language related to Turkish. Other groups, such as the Roma—also called gypsies—blend unique traditional customs and folk culture with Russian religion and society.

Three Roma children in Saint Petersburg beg for coins from passersby. This activity has figured largely in the negative stereotype of the Roma among other Russians.

The Roma and many of Russia's other national minorities were harshly oppressed by leaders including Stalin. They were stripped of their land, their rights, and often their freedom. In the early 2000s, while some groups continue to face discrimination, many have gained new pride in their ethnic backgrounds, and associations have formed to represent the nation's ethnic groups.

Language

The Russian language is written using the Cyrillic alphabet. A forerunner of the Cyrillic alphabet, called Glagolitic, was created in the ninth century by Cyril and his brother Methodius, two priests visiting Russia as missionaries. By the tenth century, Cyrillic was in widespread use in Slavic-speaking countries. Variations on the Cyrillic alphabet are still used in Russia, Ukraine, Bulgaria, and other nearby nations. Russian Cyrillic has thirty letters.

The Russian language uses its own system of naming, with most Russians going by three names. The first is the given name. The second, called a patronymic, comes from the person's father's first name. Men and women have different patronymics. A man's ends with "-ovich" or "-evich," while a woman's ends with

WRITING IN RUSSIAN

The Cyrillic alphabet used in Russia is very different from the alphabet used by English speakers. Here are a few English words translated into Russian and written in Cyrillic, followed by their phonetic pronunciations:

hello	**привет** (pree-VYET)	
good-bye	**до свидания** (dah svee-DAHN-ya)	
teacher	**учитель** (oo-CHEE-tyel)	
student	**студент** (stoo-DYENT)	

"-ovna" or "-evna." The third name is the family name, or last name. Thus the writer Leo Tolstoy, whose father's name was Nikolay, was born Leo Nikolayevich Tolstoy, while his sister was Marya Nikolayevna Tolstoy. Most Russians talk to one another using their first names and patronymics.

While Russian is the country's official language, it is not surprising that, given the nation's many different ethnic groups, more than one hundred other languages and dialects are spoken in the Russian Federation. All students must learn Russian, but schools in the various republics and regions also teach local languages.

Education

While Russians endured many hardships during the Soviet era, Soviet schools did a very good job of teaching students to read and write. As a result, literacy in Russia is nearly 100 percent for males and 99 percent for females. Going to school is mandatory for nine years in Russia. Children begin primary education at seven years old, moving on to secondary school at age ten. Most public education is provided free of charge, but some public universities did have to begin charging

Schoolchildren in a Moscow public school study math. Public school is free to all Russian children, who begin classes at age seven.

tuition during the 1990s in order to stay open. Students enrolled in higher education get a small government stipend to help them cover expenses.

Private schools began to appear following the end of the Soviet Union, and by 1998 the nation had about 600 private schools and 250 private higher education institutions. The collapse of the Soviet Union also brought huge curriculum changes. Students were no longer required to learn according to certain political theories. Students were exposed to more unbiased histories of the country and the world than they had been during the Soviet era, and many books previously banned as anti-Soviet took their places on the Russian curriculum.

Health

For many Russians, life after the collapse of the Soviet Union has been harsh. The country is still struggling to provide enough of

A doctor at a Moscow health clinic writes out a prescription. Despite advances, the Russian health care system still struggles to meet public demand for treatment.

everything for its population, and the overall standard of living is not high. Health care in Russia is of low quality, reflected in part by an infant mortality rate of 15 deaths per 1,000 live births. This rate is more than twice that of the United States, in which 6.6 deaths take place per 1,000 live births. Another telling indicator is the fact that 75 of every 100,000 women die while giving birth, compared to 12 deaths per 100,000 in the United States.

Other health problems also continue to plague Russia. Between 1990 and 2002, men saw their average life expectancy decrease from 65 years to 59 years. The average life expectancy of women in Russia was 72 years in 2002. Drug and alcohol abuse, stress, accidents, and chronic illness have all risen in Russia. These conditions are worsened by poverty, especially for the estimated one-third of Russians living at or below the poverty line. Even many of those living above the poverty level are just making ends meet.

A DEADLY DRINK

Alcoholism and alcohol-related accidents are among the leading causes of death in Russia. When Mikhail Gorbachev came into office, he tried to change this trend. Government officials entertained without alcohol. Gorbachev also lowered liquor production, a move that greatly reduced crime and work accidents. But making alcohol illegally at home became a national industry. Thousands of people died from drinking homemade liquor or such things as perfume, antifreeze, cleaning fluid, varnish, glue, or insecticide. Nevertheless, the Gorbachev antialcohol campaign helped raise male life expectancy to its highest levels ever. (These levels have since decreased again.)

HIV/AIDS One of the gravest dangers facing Russia is HIV/AIDS. In the mid-1980s, the disease was relatively rare in the Soviet Union. The government began anti-AIDS efforts in 1987, when only a small number of cases were reported. It also set up a special investigative center to deal with the disease. But by 2001, the World Health Organization (WHO) estimated that 700,000 Russians were living with HIV/AIDS, with approximately 9,000 deaths due to the virus that year.

Russia is not prepared to deal with this looming crisis. Many Russians are not educated in how to prevent contracting HIV, and hospitals lack the resources to treat the growing number of patients who have the disease. The World Bank estimates that the disease could cost Russia billions of dollars in health care, decreased productivity, and other expenses over the coming decades.

Social Services

Despite the challenges, Russia strives to provide its people with social services. The Soviet government used to pay for all medical treatments, though health care was of inconsistent quality. Top officials in the Communist Party generally received good care, but others took great risks being treated. Doctors were often unqualified and underpaid, and there were frequent shortages of medicines, vitamins, and equipment. After the collapse of the Soviet Union in 1991, things only got worse. Most people could not afford to pay market prices for medicines and treatment. In 1993 a medical insurance fund was created, paid for by employers, to help workers and their families receive the care they need.

During the years of Communism, when the Soviet government claimed to provide jobs for all workers, no unemployment or other job benefits were available. That changed after 1991, when companies and the government created a fund to provide unemployed workers with payments for up to a year. A social insurance fund paid for by

Hundreds of Russians stand in line outside the office of a state-run employment company in central Moscow. It was not until 1991 that the Russian government began to provide people with **unemployment services.**

employers was also formed to make payments for lost earnings due to sickness or pregnancy.

Retirees' pensions are provided by funds financed by company, worker, and government contributions. Pensions go to women fifty-five and older who have worked for at least twenty years and to men sixty and older who have worked for at least twenty-five years. The pension fund also pays disability payments, as well as reduced pension payments to those who don't qualify for the full amounts. Plans are also in place to create private pension funds.

Learn more about the people of Russia's republics, learn some basic Russian phrases, and find out about current issues faced by Russians at vgsbooks.com.

CULTURAL LIFE

The long history of the Russian people—filled with both glory and suffering—has produced one of the richest cultures in the world. Beginning in ancient times with simple folk arts such as woodcarving, Russia developed exquisite religious icon painting, distinctive church architecture, majestic poetry, sweeping novels, and innovative composers and dancers.

Chess, literature, and classical music are examples of arts that have long been held in great esteem by Russians. But modern culture—including rock-and-roll music, performance art, American fast-food restaurants, and television—is a growing part of everyday life in Russia, especially among young people.

Religion

The Russian Orthodox Church has been a great constant in Russian life. Founded more than one thousand years ago, it still conducts its services in Old Church Slavonic, an ancient Slavic language used for religious purposes since the 900s. Under the czars, the Russian

Orthodox Church was the nation's official church. Later, during the Soviet years, Russia was officially an atheist, or nonreligious, state. But the church survived, and the collapse of Communism led to a religious revival. In the early 2000s, the church had about 75 million members.

Other growing religions in Russia are Islam and Buddhism. Islam, with an estimated 15 million to 22 million followers, is most commonly practiced among the northern Caucasus peoples, such as the Chechens and the Ingush. It is also practiced among the Tatars, the Chuvash, and the Bashkirs of the central Volga region.

Buddhism was established in Russia in the 1700s, and before the Russian Revolution, there were more than forty monasteries throughout the country. By 1990 that number had dropped to two but went up to more than twenty as monasteries were restored or newly built. By the early 2000s, there were close to one million Buddhists in Russia. Buddhism is most widely followed by the Buryat, the Tyvan, and the Kalmyk ethnic groups.

A group of Russian Jews gather for their daily prayer around the Torah (a holy Jewish text) at the Grand Choral Synagogue in Saint Petersburg.

Judaism also has a long history in Russia, although the government considers Jews an ethnic rather than a religious group. At the beginning of the twentieth century, about half of the world's Jews lived in Russia. But they were heavily persecuted, especially during the late 1800s, when they were the victims of harsh government-organized attacks called pogroms. Mass emigration began, and millions of Jews left the country. Although the government prohibits religious persecution in modern Russia, prejudice against Jews remains. Many of the nation's Jews—an estimated population of anywhere between 400,000 and 3,000,000—seek to leave for Israel or other nations.

Holidays and Festivals

Despite the Soviet government's restrictions on religious practice and celebration, the biggest festivals in post-Communist Russia still revolve around religion. Christmas is a major holiday, but Easter, or Paskha, is the largest celebration of all. The somber season of Lent—a six-week period before Easter during which most Russian Orthodox Christians spend their time in prayer and fasting—ends with the joyous Easter Mass. Held near midnight on the night before Easter, the long church service reaches its climax when the priest carries a cross down the aisle and out the church doors. The congregation follows, singing and holding candles, and the procession circles the building three times. Then the people return to the church to find it empty, symbolizing the Easter story of Jesus rising from the tomb, leaving it for his disciples to find empty. Family and friends greet each other with three kisses on alternate cheeks and hurry home to enjoy a lavish holiday feast.

A unique event called the White Nights Festival takes place in Saint Petersburg in late June and early July. The three-hundred-year-old city is so far north that the sun barely sets during a stretch of summer known as the white nights, or *beliye nochi*. During this magical festival, the streetlights are turned off and people stroll across the city's bridges and through its streets all night long, enjoying midnight suppers and attending star-studded ballets and concerts.

In addition to these celebrations, Russians observe eleven national holidays. They include New Year's Day, International Women's Day, and Constitution Day.

Literature

The Russian literary tradition is a long and impressive one. Throughout much of their history, Russians have revered poets and writers as celebrities, idols, and legends. Native authors such as Aleksandr Pushkin, Fyodor Dostoyevsky, Leo Tolstoy, Anton Chekhov, Nikolay Gogol, Maksim Gorky, and Aleksandr Solzhenitsyn are among the best the world has ever produced.

In his time, the poet Pushkin, who also wrote short stories and plays, was as admired as anyone in the country. Especially noted for his imagery, Pushkin wrote such famous works as a novel in verse—*Eugene Onegin*—and the historical drama *Boris Godunov*. Another great was Dostoyevsky, whose complex novels describe dark plots and intricate characters with tortured souls. Among Dostoyevsky's most famous works are *Crime and Punishment* and *The Brothers Karamazov*.

Tolstoy, a nobleman, is widely thought of as Russia's greatest novelist. He wrote the epic *War and Peace*, which describes Russia at the time of Napoleon's invasion, and *Anna Karenina*, a tragic love story. During

PUSHKIN'S PASTORAL

Chased by the rays of spring,
Down the surrounding hills
    the snows already
Have run in turbid streams
Onto the flooded
    meadows. . . .
Turning blue, the heavens
    glisten.
The yet transparent woods
Come out in green as with a
    down. . . .
The lowlands dry and put on
    colors;
Herds rustle, and the
    nightingale
Has sung already in the hush
    of nights.

—from *Eugene Onegin*
by Aleksandr Pushkin

the late 1800s, the works of Anton Chekhov were also popular, including the plays *The Seagull* and *The Cherry Orchard.*

With so many literary greats, the nineteenth century was considered the golden age of Russian literature. In the early twentieth century, the onset of Communism and its strict censorship rules made it more difficult for writers to express themselves freely. However, the country continued to produce great writers. Maksim Gorky grew up as the empire was dying. When the Communists first came to power, Gorky embraced their idea of socialist realism. This school of literature and art focused on using realistic (rather than abstract) artistic expression to portray events and to praise the Soviet system. Among Gorky's works are *Mother* and *The Lower Depths.* Other writers, however, came into conflict with the government's ideas of art. Boris Pasternak, who wrote *Doctor Zhivago,* and Aleksandr Solzhenitsyn, who wrote *The Gulag Archipelago,* both had their books banned. Despite their struggles for recognition in their own country, both Pasternak and Solzhenitsyn won the Nobel Prize for literature.

Maksim Gorky

Music and Dance

The earliest Russian music was folk music, which used such instruments as the stringed balalaika and *domra.* By the nineteenth century, Russian music had grown from these roots to be among the best in the world. One of the country's most famous classical composers was Pyotr Tchaikovsky. Considered by many to be the greatest Russian

A troupe of folk musicians plays at a local harvest festival in western Russia. Folk music and folk dance remain important parts of Russia's national identity.

composer, Tchaikovsky created works—including the ballets *Swan Lake*, *Sleeping Beauty*, and *The Nutcracker*—that are still produced worldwide. Mikhail Glinka, a composer who based his work on folk tunes and national themes, also had a distinguished career. Among other accomplishments, he wrote the music used for one of Russia's national anthems.

In the early twentieth century, Igor Stravinsky continued the great Russian music tradition. He was known for creating jarring, modern pieces, which sometimes shocked his audiences. Stravinsky's *Rite of Spring* is considered a turning point in modern music, and among his other famous works are *The Firebird*, *Petrushka*, and the controversial *Svadebka (The Little Wedding)*. Sergey Rachmaninoff, who wrote in a romantic style, also became a giant of twentieth-century music with his innovative piano work. After the Communists came to power, both Rachmaninoff and Stravinksy left Russia.

Alongside its great music, Russia fostered a great ballet tradition in the nineteenth century. By the twentieth century, Russian ballet dancers were being acclaimed as among the very best in the world. Sergey Diaghilev, who founded the Ballets Russes in 1909, is credited with propelling Russian ballet to the top. Renowned composers including Stravinksy wrote works for the Ballets Russes, further increasing its prestige.

The Bolshoi Ballet in Moscow and the Maryinsky Ballet (formerly the Kirov) in Saint Petersburg remain modern Russia's most famous ballet companies. Among the stars they have produced are Vaslav Nijinsky, Anna Pavlova, Rudolf Nureyev, and Mikhail Baryshnikov.

A Maryinsky Ballet dancer twirls gracefully on a Saint Petersburg stage. Many of the world's most famous ballet dancers were born and trained in Russia.

Many of the great Russian dancers eventually defected from, or left, the Soviet Union for the United States or Europe to be free of the Communist government's restrictions.

◉ Visual Arts and Architecture

One of the earliest Russian art forms, introduced in the tenth century, was the creation of religious icons. These beautiful images of saints and other holy figures were painted on wood and displayed in churches and homes. Frescoes (paintings done directly on wet plastered walls) were also widely used in churches and palaces. Later, when Peter the Great began his crusade to modernize Russia, he encouraged Russian artists to embrace European ideas of art. This influence led many Russian painters to begin creating grand portraits and landscapes.

After Communism replaced the monarchy, art was seen by the Soviet government as a way to mirror the realities of society. Russian painters were expected to use socialist realism to express the grand nature of the revolution and its leaders in a realistic style. Millions of portraits and statues of Lenin and Stalin were created and placed throughout the country. Some artists, including Aleksandr Rodchenko, embraced socialist realism. Others, such as Wassily Kandinsky and Marc Chagall, came into conflict with the government

Statues of former Soviet heads of state lie in disrepair in a Moscow park. During Communist rule, the government commissioned many such artistic works.

for their individuality and ended up leaving the country. Others weathered the storm of Communism and enjoyed new freedoms after the breakup of the Soviet Union. The collapse loosened artistic restraints, allowing abstract painting to reemerge and paving the way for performance art and various experimental forms to develop in major Russian cities.

A Russian Orthodox church

The builders of Russian churches developed much of the nation's most distinctive architecture. The Russian Orthodox Church began as an offshoot of the Greek Orthodox Church, but it soon developed its own architectural style. For example, Russians use a pointed, or onion-shaped, dome to top their churches instead of the flatter dome favored by the Greek Orthodox Church. The onion shape may have been adopted because it allows snow to fall off faster and more easily— an important feature, given the severity of the Russian winter. Windows in Russian churches also tend to be smaller than those in Greek churches, again because of the harsh winters.

Outside influences on architecture can also be seen throughout the country. During imperial times, it was not unusual for the czars to hire European architects and artisans to build their palaces and to decorate their homes. When Peter the Great built Saint Petersburg, he relied on the famous Italian architect Bartolomeo Rastrelli. Rastrelli's most famous Russian work is the giant Winter Palace. French culture and style, at its height when Peter was in power, also had a great effect on Russian architecture and painting. This impact lessened after Napoleon's invasion, as Russian artists began looking at their own country for inspiration.

Soviet architecture reflected the political philosophies of the times. Individual expression was discouraged, while realism and utility were encouraged. Buildings were supposed to be functional, not beautiful, and huge, flat buildings of concrete were erected. These massive structures both dwarfed the individual and demonstrated the power of the government. Moscow's Seven Sisters, seven skyscrapers built by Stalin, provide one of the most famous examples of this architectural style.

Sports and Recreation

Sports, especially in the latter half of the twentieth century, played an important role in the life of most Russians. The Soviet government's desire to prove its superiority extended to the playing field, and money was poured into creating better and better athletes. Youngsters who showed athletic promise were sent to special schools and given special training. The training could be harsh, and the pressure to succeed sometimes led to the use of steroids or other illegal drugs. But Olympic stardom often provided homes and education for athletes' families. Gymnasts such as Olga Korbut and figure skaters such as Ekaterina Gordeeva and Sergey Grinkov became international stars. However, Russia lost many of its stars after the collapse of the Soviet

Gordeeva and Grinkov

Union, and some of the region's most outstanding athletes continue to hail from republics including Ukraine and Belarus. The Soviet Union also produced champions in sports such as hockey, weight lifting, and basketball, and Moscow hosted the 1980 Summer Olympics.

Professional sports have not played a major role in Russian life. However, the country has recently joined much of the world in an obsession with soccer, and the Russian team qualified to play in the 2002 World Cup. Hockey, basketball, and chess are also favorite pastimes. Another great treat is going to the circus, which has been popular in Russia since the time of Catherine the Great.

▶ Food

The hearty Russian diet is loaded with bread, potatoes, and meats, often topped with thick, warm sauces to ward off winter's chill. Some of Russia's classic dishes,

A Moscow street vendor sells rolls, cookies, and **bread.** Starchy foods such as bread and potatoes are staples of the Russian diet.

such as borscht (beet soup) and beef Stroganoff, are favorites world-wide. One of the best known Russian foods is caviar, the eggs of the sturgeon fish. A highly prized delicacy, caviar can be very expensive.

Vodka is one of the best known Russian drinks, and many Russians drink it with meals. But tea drinking is also a great part of Russian daily life, and the family samovar—a metal urn that may be simply or ornately decorated—is a treasured possession in nearly every Russian household.

BORSCHT

Borscht, a soup made primarily of beets, is one of the most popular dishes in Russia. It reportedly appeared at the end of the eighteenth century. During hard times, Russians often make borscht only with vegetables, while in better days they may choose to use meat as well.

2 beets

2 carrots

1 onion, peeled and halved

12 c. canned beef broth

3 medium potatoes, peeled

¼ head green cabbage

1 tbsp. dried parsley flakes

¼ tsp. salt

1 tsp. lemon juice

pepper to taste

sour cream and fresh dill to garnish

1. Wash beets and carrots thoroughly. Place beets, one carrot, and onion in a large stockpot. Add 11 cups beef broth and bring to a boil over high heat. Reduce heat to medium and use a ladle or skim off any foam that forms on the surface. Cook for 20 to 25 minutes, or until vegetables are soft.
2. Remove vegetables from pot. Discard onion and set carrot and beets aside to cool.
3. Cut potatoes into quarters. Slice cabbage into strips. Peel and slice raw carrot. Add potatoes, cabbage, raw carrot, parsley, salt, and remaining 1 cup broth to pot. Cook for 30 minutes.
4. Peel cooked beets and cooked carrot, grate or chop finely, and add to soup. Cook 10 to 15 minutes longer.
5. Add lemon juice and pepper and stir. Serve borscht hot with sour cream and dill.

Serves 6.

THE ECONOMY

Russia's economy has had its share of struggles over the years. The nation's huge population, vast expanses, and harsh winters have frequently made it difficult to distribute resources throughout the country. Under the rule of the czars, the economy relied heavily on the work of agricultural peasants, and one season of failed crops could plunge the nation into devastating famine. The Soviet government's series of Five-Year Plans were intended to stabilize the economy but brought little relief—and sometimes even greater suffering. The fall of the Soviet Union in 1991 brought Russia's economy to the brink of collapse. According to the World Bank, the country's gross domestic product, or GDP—the value of goods and services produced within a country's borders—fell from more than $1 trillion in 1990 to less than $200 billion by the end of the century.

This dizzying decline produced economic instability and social discontent. Inflation (rising prices combined with a decline in the value of national currency) hit double- and at times triple-digit levels

during the 1990s. Prices for goods from toilet paper to shoes increased dramatically, and the value of the ruble, Russia's national currency, plummeted. Soviet citizens had grown used to the government providing such basic things as food and shelter, and many people found that they could not afford both in the new economy. To raise money, Russians sold everything from their furniture to their pets on the streets.

This financial crisis opened the door to widespread corruption and organized crime as people struggled to survive. Russia's economy was finally beginning to rebound by 2001, as the GDP grew to more than $310 billion. But about one-third of the population was still living at or below the poverty line. Estimates put Russia's per capita income at $8,010 per year, less than half of the European average. The nation's official unemployment rate is about 10 percent. However, there is a great deal of underemployment, with many of the 65 million people in the workforce only able to obtain part-time jobs or to do work for which they are overqualified.

A homeless woman covers her dog with her coat. They live in a shantytown near the Kremlin. Poverty and homelessness have been problems in Russia since the fall of the Soviet Union.

Over time, the relative importance of Russia's economic sectors has shifted significantly. In imperial days, Russia had an agricultural society and economy. By the 1940s and 1950s, Stalin's push for power had forced the country to industrialize. During the remainder of the twentieth century, the industrial sector was the nation's dominant employer. In the early twenty-first century, services have grown to be the most important area of the Russian economy.

Services, Industry, and Energy

The growing importance of the service sector—which includes workers such as salespeople, hotel staff, mechanics, and tour guides—provides a dramatic indication of how the Russian economy has changed and is still changing. In 1990, when the Soviet Union was nearing its collapse, the services sector contributed only 36 percent of Russia's GDP. In 2000, however, services contributed about 55 percent of the nation's GDP, providing about 59 percent of jobs in the economy—close to twice the number of jobs found in industry. The biggest growth in the new economy has been in areas such as insurance, real estate, banking, and finance. In addition, many new stores, malls, restaurants, and small businesses have sprung up all over the country.

Industry, which includes manufacturing, energy, and mining, has slipped to become the second largest area of the Russian GDP, contributing about 35 percent in 2000. Nevertheless, Russia remains an industrial power. The government estimated that 150,000 industrial enterprises operated in Russia at the beginning of 2002.

The Russian manufacturing sector is by far the biggest employer in industry. In 2000 it employed more than 11 million people, who made goods such as food products, machinery, iron and steel, transportation equipment, and chemical products. Russian plants produce everything from jet airplanes and space vehicles to tractors and televisions.

The energy sector also remains a huge part of the Russian economy. Russia has the largest natural gas reserves in the world and is the leading exporter of the fuel. The industry is so important that Gazprom, the state-run natural gas company, operates 90,000 miles (144,837 km) of pipelines and employs thousands of people. In addition, Russia's thirty nuclear reactors provide about 15 percent of the country's power. There have been several severe nuclear accidents, but no plans are in place to eliminate any of the reactors. In fact, the country is hoping to build more by 2005.

Russia also operates coal- and oil-powered plants. With some 150 billion tons (136 billion metric tons) of coal reserves—a resource second only to the U.S. reserves in size—coal accounts for about 16 percent of the power generated in Russia. Russia also is one of the leading oil producers in the world, along with the United States and Saudi Arabia. Mineral resources including bauxite, cobalt, copper, diamonds, gold, iron ore, nickel, platinum, and tin keep Russia's mining industry busy.

Agriculture, Forestry, and Fishing

Despite Russia's size, only about one-tenth of its territory is suitable for farming, a shortage that has resulted in severe famines and millions of deaths. The inefficiency of collective farms under the Soviet government only made the problem worse. In post-Communist Russia, where private ownership of land is a relatively new concept, investment in the agricultural sector has lagged.

A family harvests their yearly crop of potatoes on **a privately owned farm.** Russian investors remain wary of noncollective land ownership, so the agricultural sector of the economy is sluggish.

Little of Russia's land is fertile enough to farm, but crops such as **sugar beets** are hardy enough to thrive.

Still, after years of struggle, the Russian government reported large harvests in 2000 and 2001. Agriculture, combined with forestry, accounts for about 7 percent of the country's GDP, providing more than 7 million workers with jobs. The nation's main agricultural products are grains, potatoes, sugar beets, and livestock. According to Russian estimates, good years can produce harvests of more than 30 million tons (27 million metric tons) each of wheat and potatoes and 10 million tons (9 million metric tons) of sugar beets, along with significant amounts of meat and dairy products.

Forestry remains another important component of the Russian economy. Given the size of its forests, it is not surprising that Russia has the largest wood reserves in the world. In 2001 it produced more than 5 million tons (4.5 million metric tons) of wood pulp products and a similar amount of paper and cardboard products. Russia also exported more than 4 million tons (3.6 million metric tons) of sawn wood.

Fishing is another great source of income. The country nets great catches of fish each year, including herring, salmon, and walleye. In

Sturgeon eggs, or **caviar**, are a delicacy in many countries. Russian fishers provide consumers with 90 percent of the world's caviar.

GOLDEN EGGS

Caviar is one of the most famous Russian foods. It is also one of the most expensive. Caviar is considered a luxury and can cost more than $500 per pound. Caviar comes from the eggs of sturgeon and is sold in red and black varieties. However, toxic chemicals that pollute the water have reduced Russia's sturgeon catch by almost 60 percent since the early 1990s, dramatically affecting caviar production and sales.

2001 Russia reported exports exceeding 800,000 tons (725,760 metric tons) of fresh and frozen fish.

Foreign Trade

Another indication of the Russian economy's recovery is the country's balance of imports and exports. In 1999 the World Bank reported that Russia registered a trade surplus of nearly $34 million, having exported a greater value of goods than it imported. That surplus increased to more than $58 billion in 2000, boding well for the future.

Some of Russia's main customers for exports are the United States, Germany, Ukraine, Belarus, and Italy. The chief exports from Russia are natural gas, oil, metals, and timber. Russia imports the most goods from Germany, Belarus, Ukraine, the United States, and Kazakhstan. Major imports include machinery, meat, sugar, and medicines.

Illegal Activities

One of the thorniest problems with an unstable economy is that many people may be driven to make money any way they can—legally or otherwise. The new Russia is no exception, as corruption and organized crime have formed a growing segment of the economy since the Soviet Union's collapse. The government estimates that as much as

40 percent of the GDP, or more than $100 billion, is being lost to corruption or illegal activities. Hundreds of crime rings operate in the country, some of them supported or protected by corrupt government officials. The rings' activities include theft, blackmail, and murder. The government estimates that crime rings have taken over or influenced thousands of companies and government enterprises.

Drug use is also a problem, as people use illegal drugs both as an escape and as a means of making money. According to law enforcement agencies, Russia itself is being used more and more as a transfer point for illegal drugs going to other countries. Another major concern involves the thousands of nuclear weapons that remained in the nation when the Soviet Union broke up. Some observers fear that terrorists, organized criminals, or even corrupt government officials might steal and then sell atomic weapons or nuclear material to unfriendly governments or individuals.

The Future

The difficult times of the 1990s seem like a distant memory to many people in Russia. Gone are the days of triple-digit inflation, when the ruble's value sank as low as six thousand rubles to one dollar. Having survived such bad times, Russia has become an increasingly attractive place to do business. The inflation rate is finally manageable, the country's financial markets have stabilized, and steady economic growth is forecast for the future.

Other numbers also show that the economy is improving. Russia's debt is dropping, having fallen from $158 billion in 1998 to about $137 billion in 2001. Foreign investments in the country are on the increase, approaching $5 billion in 2002, compared to less than $2 billion in 1998. Economists estimate that the GDP grew about 5.1 percent in 2001—a sharp contrast to the GDP's average decrease of 6.1 percent each year from 1990 to 1999. Russia's new growth is expected to continue for several more years.

> The official rate of exchange was once one ruble to one U.S. dollar. In the late 1990s, hyperinflation reduced the ruble's value so dramatically that the exchange rate reached almost six thousand rubles to one dollar. To raise the ruble's worth, the Russian government revalued the currency, making one new ruble equal to one thousand of the old rubles. In 2003 the exchange rate was about thirty new rubles to one U.S. dollar.

Visit vgsbooks.com for up-to-date information about Russia's economy and a converter where you can learn how many Russian rubles are in a U.S. dollar.

In addition, Russia's president Vladimir Putin has stressed the importance of small businesses as an engine of the economy. Small businesses only provide about 10 percent of the GDP, at about $25 billion—a small amount compared to ratios in other industrialized countries. Putin hopes that small businesses will account for about half of the GDP by 2005. This development, along with other reforms, could help get Russia firmly back on its feet after a long, hard road.

The benefits of an improved economy could also have a ripple effect through the entire society. Better standards of living may strengthen democracy in the country and boost the talents and innovation of the people. Russians hope that all of these factors will combine to transform their nation into a new, modern society that also has the benefit of a long, rich history.

The **Russian flag** flies proudly above the Volga River. The flag is a symbol of hope for many Russians, representing the promise of a brighter future.

Timeline

A.D 860	The Cyrillic alphabet is developed.
862	Rurik becomes ruler of Novgorod and lays the foundations for Kievan Rus.
988	Prince Vladimir creates the Russian Orthodox Church.
1030	The first school is started in Novgorod.
1054-1073	Russkaia Pravda, the first Russian laws, are written.
1116	*The Primary Chronicle*, a history of early Russia, is composed.
1237-1242	The Mongols take control of Russia.
1294	The first dated and signed Russian icon is produced in Novgorod.
1462	Ivan the Great becomes ruler of Russia.
1533	Ivan the Terrible becomes the ruler of Russia.
1564	The first Russian book is printed in Moscow.
1598	The Time of Troubles begins.
1613	The Romanov dynasty begins with Czar Mikhail Romanov.
1682	Peter the Great becomes czar, sharing the duties with his brother.
1695	Peter the Great forms the Russian navy.
1703	Russia's first newspaper is established. Saint Petersburg is built.
1725	The Academy of Sciences is founded in Saint Petersburg.
1762	Catherine the Great becomes ruler.
1773	A major peasant rebellion, led by the serf Pugachov, begins.
1812	Napoleon is defeated following his invasion of Russia.
1825	Nicholas I becomes czar. The Decembrist revolt fails.
1861	Czar Alexander II frees the serfs.
1868	Leo Tolstoy's *War and Peace* is published.
1877	Pyotr Tchaikovsky's *Swan Lake* premieres.
1891	The construction of the Trans-Siberian Railroad begins.
1894	Nicholas II becomes czar.
1904-1905	Russo-Japanese War takes place.

1905   The Bloody Sunday protest leaves hundreds dead.

1906   The first Russian constitution is written.

1913   Igor Stravinsky's *Rite of Spring* debuts in Paris.

1914   World War I begins.

1917   Czar Nicholas II gives up his throne, and the Bolsheviks take power.

1918   Russia exits World War I. The Bolsheviks execute Nicholas II and his family. Russia adopts the Gregorian calendar.

1921   Lenin introduces his New Economic Policy.

1922   The Union of Soviet Socialist Republics (USSR) is formed.

1927   Joseph Stalin assumes control.

1939-1945   World War II takes place.

1946   The Cold War begins.

1949   The Soviets build an atomic bomb.

1957   *Sputnik I* is launched into space.

1958   Boris Pasternak is awarded the Nobel Prize for literature.

1961   Cosmonaut Yury Gagarin becomes the first human in space. The Berlin Wall is built.

1962   The Cuban Missile Crisis takes place.

1970   Aleksandr Solzhenitsyn wins the Nobel Prize for literature

1979   Soviet troops invade Afghanistan.

1985   Mikhail Gorbachev takes power.

1990   Gorbachev wins the Nobel Peace Prize. The first McDonald's Restaurant in Russia opens in Moscow.

1991   Boris Yeltsin is elected president of Russia. The Soviet Union collapses.

1992   The Russian Federation is created.

1994   Russian troops invade the Republic of Chechnya.

2000   Vladimir Putin is elected president of Russia.

2002   Chechen terrorists take hostages in a Moscow theater.

2003   Twin suicide bombings at a Moscow concert kill more than one dozen people. The bombers are believed to be Chechen terrorists.

COUNTRY NAME Russian Federation (Rossiiskaya Federatsiya)

AREA 6,592,692 square miles (17,075,072 sq. km)

MAIN LANDFORMS West Siberian Plain, Central Siberian Plateau, East Siberian Uplands, Ural Mountains, Caucasus Mountains, tundra, taiga, steppes, desert

HIGHEST POINT Mount Elbrus, 18,510 feet (5,642 m) above sea level

LOWEST POINT Caspian Sea, 92 feet (28 m) below sea level

MAJOR RIVERS Volga, Don, Ob, Yenisey, Irtysh, Lena, Amur

ANIMALS Amur leopards, bison, brown bears, deer, minks, polar bears, reindeer, sables, seals, tigers, wolverines

CAPITAL CITY Moscow

OTHER MAJOR CITIES Saint Petersburg, Novgorod, Novosibirsk, Nizhniy Novgorod, Volgograd, Vladivostok

OFFICIAL LANGUAGE Russian

MONETARY UNIT Ruble. 1 ruble = 100 kopecks.

RUSSIAN CURRENCY

The ruble is the official currency of Russia. One ruble is equal to one hundred kopecks. Kopecks come in denominations of one, five, ten, and fifty. In the nation's early history, Russians used gold and silver coins to buy and sell goods. When these metals became hard to get in the twelfth century, people used fur or other valuable items as money. The ruble emerged in the fourteenth century, and it has existed in various forms since then.

The Russian flag consists of three horizontal bars of white, blue, and red. The flag was first adopted in 1799. Following the 1917 Russian Revolution, it was replaced with the Communist flag that featured a hammer and sickle. The present flag was reintroduced in 1991 after the Soviet Union collapsed. There are several theories regarding the flag's symbolism. One story states that the three bars represent God (white), the czar (blue), and the people (red). Boris Yeltsin established Flag Day on August 22, 1994, marking the first time in Russia's history that such a holiday existed.

When the Soviet Union collapsed in 1991, the Russian Federation needed a new anthem. Yeltsin chose Mikhail Glinka's "Patriotic Song," composed in the 1800s, but the wordless anthem never became popular. Many Russians wanted to return to the old Soviet anthem. Its melody was inspiring, but its lyrics praised the Communist system. In 2000 President Vladimir Putin approved an anthem with the music of an old Soviet anthem, composed by Aleksandr Alexandrov. Revised lyrics were written by Sergey Mikhalkov—the same man who had written lyrics to the Soviet anthem in 1944. The anthem's first verse and refrain follow:

Anthem of Russia
Russia, our holy country!
Russia, our beloved country!
A mighty will, a great glory,
Are your inheritance for all time!

Be glorious, our free Fatherland!
Eternal union of fraternal peoples,
Common wisdom given by our forebears,
Be glorious, our country! We are proud of you!
From the southern seas to the polar region
spread our forests and fields.
You are unique in the world, inimitable,
Native land protected by God!

For a link where you can listen to the Russian national anthem, go to vgsbooks.com.

Famous People

CATHERINE THE GREAT (1729–1796) At the age of sixteen, Princess Sophie Friederike Auguste von Anhalt-Zerbst of Prussia took the name Catherine and married Peter the Great's grandson, who later became Czar Peter III. Their marriage was unhappy, and Peter was overthrown. Eight days later, he was assassinated (many people believe by his ambitious wife). Catherine was proclaimed empress of Russia. She ruled for thirty-four years.

MIKHAIL GORBACHEV (b. 1931) Gorbachev was the last leader of the Soviet Union. A native of the Caucasus region, he worked to promote disarmament, to crack down on corruption, and to reduce alcoholism. Gorbachev won the 1990 Nobel Peace Prize for his role in ending the Cold War, but his changes ultimately contributed to the USSR's collapse.

EKATERINA GORDEEVA (b. 1971) Born in Moscow, Gordeeva began figure skating when she was four years old. She went on to skate with Sergey Grinkov. Gordeeva and Grinkov, who were eventually married, won two Olympic gold medals and many other awards. After Grinkov's death of a heart attack in 1995, Gordeeva continued to skate. One of her most memorable solo performances was a tribute to Grinkov's memory.

VLADIMIR ILICH LENIN (1870–1924) Born Vladimir Ulyanov in Simbirsk, a city on the southern Volga, Lenin is considered the father of the Russian Revolution and the Soviet Union. He became a revolutionary after his older brother was hanged for plotting to kill the czar. In 1900 he changed his name to Lenin after Siberia's Lena River. Lenin died in 1924, and his body remains in a tomb in Red Square.

IVAN PAVLOV (1849–1936) Born in Ryazan, a town southwest of Moscow, Pavlov was a psychologist who studied conditioned responses in dogs. Pavlov sounded bells at dinnertime, and eventually the dogs learned to salivate at the sound of the bell whether they got food or not. Pavlov won the 1904 Nobel Prize for physiology or medicine for his work.

ANNA PAVLOVA (1881–1931) As a girl growing up in Saint Petersburg, Pavlova dreamed of being a dancer. By the time she was ten years old, she was enrolled at the Imperial School of the Maryinsky Ballet. She went on to travel the globe and to found her own ballet company, becoming one of the most admired ballerinas in Europe and around the world. Pavlova was most famous for her rendition of *The Dying Swan*.

PETER THE GREAT (1672–1725) Born in Moscow, Peter is considered one of the greatest Russian czars. He sought to modernize and Europeanize all areas of Russian life. He created a strong navy, reorganized the army, secularized schools, and took greater control over the church. He also recruited scientific experts, modernized the Russian alphabet, introduced the Julian calendar, and established the first Russian newspaper.

ALEKSANDR PUSHKIN (1799–1837) Russia's most famous poet, Pushkin was born in Moscow. He is often called the father of Russian literature, and many Russians can quote his poems by heart. Despite his popularity among the people, Pushkin was exiled in 1824 because some of his writings were considered revolutionary and sacrilegious. At the age of thirty-seven, he was killed in a duel defending his wife's honor.

GRIGORY RASPUTIN (1872–1916) A self-proclaimed religious healer from Siberia, Rasputin gained influence over the imperial family—and over Czar Nicholas II's government—after convincing Empress Alexandra that he could treat her son's blood condition. Determined to eliminate this influence, a group of Russian aristocrats invited Rasputin to a deadly dinner. When the poisoned cakes and tea consumed by Rasputin did not affect him, his assassins shot him and threw him into a freezing river.

JOSEPH STALIN (1878–1953) Stalin was born Iosif Dzhugashvili in Gori, Georgia (a former Soviet republic). He chose the name Stalin based on the Russian word *stal*, meaning "steel." Stalin was responsible for killing an estimated 20 million or more of his fellow citizens, and he was absolute ruler of the Soviet Union for almost thirty years. He often said that he trusted no one, not even himself.

IGOR STRAVINSKY (1882–1971) Stravinsky was born in Oranienbaum, southwest of Saint Petersburg, to a father who expected his son to work in government. Instead, Stravinsky became a modern composer who often shocked audiences with his daring works. Stravinsky's first significant composition was the orchestral piece *Fireworks* (1908). His ballets *The Firebird* (1910), *Petrushka* (1911), and *Rite of Spring* (1912–1913) scandalized audiences of the time but became classics.

LEO TOLSTOY (1828–1910) Born to a noble family on a rural estate near Moscow, Tolstoy tried his hand as a lawyer, a soldier, and a teacher before he became one of the most famous writers in Russian history. His most famous work, *War and Peace,* was completed in 1869, and he finished his masterpiece *Anna Karenina* ten years later. Near the end of his life, Tolstoy sought spiritual enlightenment and social justice.

MARINA TSVETAYEVA (1892–1941) Born in Moscow, Tsvetayeva began writing poetry as a child. She published a significant amount of poetry in Russia until the 1920s, when her work was banned by the Soviet government as anti-Communist. However, Tsvetayeva continued to write from abroad. She returned to the USSR in 1938 but was still targeted as an enemy of the state. After her husband was executed and her daughter was forced into a labor camp, Tsvetayeva committed suicide.

GUM Located in Moscow, GUM used to be the biggest department store in the world, but its shelves were often empty during hard times. After the fall of the Soviet Union, the store was converted to a shopping mall. GUM, pronounced "gay-oo-em," stands for Gosudarstvenni Universalnyi Magazin, or state department store.

THE HERMITAGE Located in Saint Petersburg, the Hermitage is one of the world's great museums with more than three million pieces on display. The art was once the private collection of the czars. One particularly prized area is the Treasure Gallery, which exhibits a collection of gold, silver, and jewels. There are also pieces from prehistoric times to the twentieth century.

KAMCHATKA PENINSULA Located on the eastern coast of Russia, this peninsula is one of the most beautiful and harshest places on earth. It is filled with geysers and volcanoes and is also subject to earthquakes.

THE KREMLIN Located in Moscow, the Kremlin is the original fortress around which Moscow was built. It houses the government of Russia, as well as monuments, churches, and exhibits, including the world's largest cannon and the world's largest bell.

LAKE BAIKAL Located in Siberia, Baikal is the deepest lake on earth and home to about two thousand species of plants and animals. The water is so clear that visitors can see far into the lake's depths.

LENIN'S TOMB Located in Moscow, this pyramid-like granite mausoleum holds the body of V. I. Lenin. The body was placed at its Red Square location in 1924, and hundreds of visitors come to the tomb each week. It is forbidden to carry cameras inside.

THE TRANS-SIBERIAN RAILROAD One of the engineering marvels of the world, the railroad travels more than 5,000 miles (8,047 km) across Siberia from Vladivostok on the Pacific Coast to Moscow. The trip takes more than 150 hours. The railroad, completed in 1916, took more than thirteen years to build and has close to three hundred stations.

THE WINTER PALACE Located in Saint Petersburg, the Winter Palace is one of the largest buildings in the world. The former home of the czars, it has more than one thousand rooms and two thousand windows and is large enough to house the entire Hermitage. The roof of this ornate building is adorned with statues.

arms race: a competition between the Soviets and the United States to see who could build the strongest military in the world. The two countries spent billions of dollars on soldiers, tanks, planes, ships, rockets, bombs, and nuclear weapons.

capitalism: an economic system in which private ownership prevails and making money is the goal. Prices are theoretically set by the market in open competition.

Cold War: a phrase used to describe the competition, which was short of war, between the United States and the Soviet Union that developed after World War II. Both sides tried to dominate the world with their political and economic systems.

Communism: a system of government in which the state plans and controls everything for the benefit of the workers while also working toward a higher social order. The system is based on the writings of the German economist Karl Marx.

czar: an all-powerful emperor of Russia. The czar's oldest son usually inherited the throne from his father.

Five-Year Plan: an economic forecast developed by Stalin in which the government set ambitious production goals for the agricultural and industrial sectors to meet. The Five-Year Plans helped transform the Soviet Union into a world superpower.

glasnost: a concept coined by Mikhail Gorbachev. It means openness and was intended to show that the Soviet government would discuss social problems and shortcomings.

perestroika: a Gorbachev-created concept meant to change the way the Communist Party and the economy operated. The word literally means "restructuring." The idea behind perestroika was to modernize the nation by allowing some private ownership but to keep the Communist Party intact.

pogrom: an organized and usually government-sanctioned massacre of a certain group, usually Jews. Several of these attacks took place in Russia in the late nineteenth and early twentieth centuries. The pogroms led to widespread prejudice even after they were stopped.

serfdom: a system of forced labor. Russian serfs were peasants forced to live on the estates of the rich. They were fed and housed in exchange for their labor but were considered the property of landowners.

soviet: a council that formed the basis of society under the Communist Party. The soviets were organized in a pyramid structure, with local soviets as the base and the Supreme Soviet at the top. Each soviet was meant to make decisions that were best for its area.

Europa World Yearbook, 2001. London: Europa Publications, 2001.
Covering Russia's recent history, economy, and government, this annual publication also provides a wealth of statistics on population, employment, trade, and more.

Hosking, Geoffrey. *Russia: People and Empire 1552–1917.*
Cambridge, MA: Harvard University Press, 1997.
This book offers a straightforward account of Russia's political, social, and cultural history.

———. *Russia and the Russians: A History.* Cambridge, MA: Harvard University Press, 2001.
This comprehensive look at Russia's history examines the roles of climate and geography in the nation's past. It also looks at the history of reform, censorship, and expansion from A.D. 626 through the election of Vladimir Putin in 2000.

Marx, Karl, and Friedrich Engels. *The Communist Manifesto.* New York: Washington Square Press, 1964.
This important work was the blueprint from which the Soviet Union was built.

Mickiewicz, Ellen. *Changing Channels: Television and the Struggle for Power in Russia.* Durham, NC: Duke University Press, 1999.
This title examines how television influenced daily life in Russia during the tumultuous 1990s.

"PRB 2001 World Population Data Sheet." *Population Reference Bureau (PRB).* 2001.
<http://www.prb.org> (January 3, 2003).
This annual statistics sheet provides a wealth of data on Russia's population, birth and death rates, fertility rate, infant mortality rate, and other useful demographic information.

Reed, John. *Ten Days That Shook the World.* New York: Modern Library, 1960.
This unique journalistic look at the Russian Revolution was written by a U.S. citizen who witnessed the event.

Remnick, David. *Lenin's Tomb: The Last Days of the Soviet Empire.* New York: Vintage Books, 1994.
This must-read book, which won the Pulitzer Prize, looks at the fall of the Soviet Union and how people suffered as a result of the oppressive system.

———. *Resurrection: The Struggle for a New Russia.* New York: Vintage Books, 1998.
This companion book to *Lenin's Tomb* updates the story of the country's struggle, focusing on the new order in Russia, how the elite have adapted to marketing, and organized crime.

Shoemaker, M. Wesley. *Russia and the Commonwealth of Independent States 2001.* **Harpers Ferry, WV: Stryker-Post Publications, 2001.**
This book offers a highly detailed yet readable study of Russian history, economy, and society.

Smith, Hedrick. *The New Russians.* **New York: Avon Books, 1991.**
An update of *The Russians,* this book focuses on Gorbachev, the revolutionary changes he brings, and people's experiences as their world is ending.

———. *The Russians.* **New York: Times Books, 1983.**
This riveting book, by a Pulitzer-Prize winning author, offers an inside look at the Soviet Union during the Brezhnev years. Smith traveled the country talking to people.

Solzhenitsyn, Aleksandr. *The Gulag Archipelago 1918–1956.* **New York: Harper & Row, 1978.**
In this personal account of life in Stalin's labor camps, Solzhenitsyn talks to hundreds of prisoners and describes interrogations, torture, and hopelessness.

Turner, Barry, ed. *The Statesman's Yearbook: The Politics, Cultures, and Economies of the World, 2002.* **New York: Macmillan Press, 2001.**
This resource provides concise information on Russian history, climate, government, economy, and culture, including relevant statistics.

Wilson, Andrew, and Nina Bachkatov. *Russia and the Commonwealth A to Z.* **New York: HarperPerennial, 1992.**
This title provides easy-to-digest snippets of information, presented alphabetically. The pieces were collected by two journalists just as the Soviet Union broke up.

Further Reading and Websites

Allman, Barbara. *Dance of the Swan: A Story About Anna Pavlova.* **Minneapolis: Carolrhoda Books, 2001.**
Follow the life of this Russian ballerina as she inspires and encourages people around the world with her exceptionally graceful and expressive dance style.

Bartleby.com
Website: <http://www.bartleby.com>
This website contains the sixth edition of the *Columbia Encyclopedia*, with an excellent section on Russia.

A Chronology of Russian History
Website: <http://www.departments.bucknell.edu/russian/chrono.html>
Part of the Bucknell University's Russian Studies Department, this website offers a thorough, incredible chronology of Russian history covering Rurik to Putin.

CIA: The World Fact Book 2002
Website: <http://www.cia.gov/cia/publications/factbook>
This site provides a wealth of information on the basic political, social, and economic infrastructure of Russia.

Corona, Laurel. *The Russian Federation.* **San Diego: Lucent Books, 2001.**
This short but comprehensive book examines the economy, politics, and daily life of Russia.

Dostoyevsky, Fyodor. *The Brothers Karamazov.* **Translated by Richard Pevear and Larissa Volokhonsky. New York: Farrar, Straus and Giroux, 2002.**
Originally published in Russian in 1880, this classic study of the spiritual and psychological struggles of a family in late nineteenth-century Russia is considered a masterpiece.

Kort, Michael. *Russia.* **New York: Facts On File, 1998.**
This book details the collapse of the Soviet Union and Russia's new road.

Plotkin, Gregory, and Rita Plotkin. *Cooking the Russian Way.* **Minneapolis: Lerner Publications Company, 2003.**
This cultural cookbook presents recipes for a variety of authentic and traditional Russian dishes, including special foods for holidays and festivals.

Popescu, Julian. *Russia.* **Philadelphia: Chelsea House Publishers, 1999.**
This title covers the basics about life in Russia.

Pushkin, Aleksandr. *Eugene Onegin: A Novel in Verse.* **Translated by Douglas Hofstadter. New York: Basic Books, 1999.**
Pushkin is Russia's most famous poet, and this famous work—originally published in Russian in 1833—depicts Russian life in the early 1800s.

Robinson, Deborah. *The Sami of Northern Europe.* **Minneapolis: Lerner Publications Company, 2002.**
This book discusses the history and culture of the Sami, one of Russia's many ethnic groups.

Toht, Patricia. *Daily Life in Ancient and Modern Moscow.* **Minneapolis: Runestone Press, 2001.**
This title takes readers on a historical tour of Russia's capital, from its founding to the present.

Tolstoy, Leo. *War and Peace.* **Translated by Constance Garnett. New York: Modern Library, 1994.**
This epic novel, originally published in Russian in the 1860s, is a dramatic story of Napoleon's invasion of Russia and its effect on the nation's people.

vgsbooks.com
Website: <http://www.vgsbooks.com>
Visit vgsbooks.com, the homepage of the Visual Geography Series®, which is updated frequently. You can get linked to all sorts of useful on-line information, including geographical, historical, demographic, cultural, and economic websites. The vgsbooks.com site is a great resource for late-breaking news and statistics.

Wilson, Neil. *Nations of the World: Russia.* **Austin, TX: Raintree Steck-Vaughn, 2000.**
This book provides good tidbits of information on Russia, presented in an appealing format.

Captions for photos appearing on cover and chapter openers:

Cover: Saint Basil's Cathedral in Moscow is one of the most famous buildings in all of Russia. This ornate building was commissioned by Ivan the Terrible and built on the edge of Red Square between 1555 and 1561.

pp. 4–5 A brown bear cub forages for food in a Siberian forest. Bears have long been a national symbol of Russia.

pp. 8–9 The Russian tundra becomes lush and colorful during the summer months, disproving the belief that Russia is contantly covered in snow.

pp. 40–41 A group of children from a folk dance group in Vladivostok

pp. 48–49 The lid of this lacquerware jewelry box depicts Saint George battling a dragon. Russian artisans are famous for creating beautiful and intricate lacquerware boxes, nesting dolls, and kitchen utensils.

pp. 58–59 A collection of Russian kopeck coins and ruble notes

Photo Acknowledgments

The images in this book are used with the permission of: © Staffan Widstrand/CORBIS, pp. 4-5; Digital Cartographics, pp. 6, 11; © Wolfgang Kaehler, www.wkaehlerphoto.com, pp. 8-9, 13, 18-19, 40-41, 61; © Wally McNamee/ CORBIS, p. 10; © Dean Conger/CORBIS, p. 12; © Ralph White/CORBIS, p. 14; © John Conrad/CORBIS, p. 16; © Wolfgang Kaehler/CORBIS, p. 17; © Francoise de Mulder/CORBIS, p. 22; Library of Congress, pp. 23, 27 (both), 30-31; Pushkin Collection/University of Wisconsin-Madison, pp. 24, 26; Independent Picture Service, pp. 25 (both), 33; The Illustrated London News and Picture Library, pp. 28 (top), 29, 32, 52 (top); © Hulton|Archive by Getty Images, p. 28 (bottom); Dwight D. Eisenhower Library, p. 34; © National Air and Space Museum, Smithsonian Institution, p. 35; © Peter Turnley/CORBIS, pp. 37, 60; © JeffGreenberg@juno.com, pp. 39, 43, 44, 54, 55, 62; © Buddy Mays/TRAVEL STOCK, pp. 42, 52 (bottom), 53, 65; © AFP/CORBIS, pp. 46-47; © Dean Conger/CORBIS, pp. 48-49; © Steve Raymer/CORBIS, p. 50; © Bohemian Nomad Picturemakers/CORBIS, p. 56 (top); © Liba Taylor/CORBIS, p. 56 (bottom); © Dallas and John Heaton/CORBIS, pp. 58-59; © Roger Ressmeyer/CORBIS, p. 63; Banknotes.com, p. 68.

Cover photo: © Wolfgang Kaehler, www.wkaehlerphoto.com.
Back cover photo: NASA.

DATE			